Same-sex marriage

Is it really the same?

Mark Christopher

DayOne

© Day One Publications 2009
First printed 2009
Reprinted 2012

ISBN 978–1–84625–163–4

British Library Cataloguing in Publication Data available

Scripture quotations taken from the **New American Standard Bible®**,
Copyright © 1960, 1962, 1963, 1968, 1971, 1972, 1973,
1975, 1977, 1995 by The Lockman Foundation
Used by permission. (www.Lockman.org)

Published by Day One Publications
Ryelands Road, Leominster, HR6 8NZ
☎ 01568 613 740 FAX 01568 611 473
email—sales@dayone.co.uk
web site—www.dayone.co.uk
North American—e-mail—sales@dayonebookstore.com
North American—web site—www.dayonebookstore.com

Cover design by Wayne McMaster
Printed by Orchard Press Cheltenham Ltd

In this timely book, Pastor Mark Christopher brings the weight of God's unchanging truth to bear on the hotly debated issue of homosexuality and same-sex marriage. Scholarly and scriptural, this concise treatment is a great resource for every concerned Christian—and we all need to be concerned.

John MacArthur Jr., Pastor-Teacher, Grace Community Church, Sun Valley, California, USA

Here is a powerful exposé and rebuttal of the arguments for same-sex marriage which will serve to arm the Christian church to make battle against the forces seeking to destroy the institution of biblical marriage. Mark Christopher presents a concise but scholarly book, pregnant with current and relevant material, which will become a tool for leader and layperson alike to understand the issues involved and to use for the defense of marriage.

Alex Montoya, The Master's Seminary, USA

Same Sex Marriage: Is it Really the Same? by Mark Christopher offers a well-thought-out and researched solid biblical answer to the question that its title raises. In this small volume he does a number of very helpful things. First, he examines and exposits key biblical passages and concepts of what God intended marriage to be. He then proceeds to expose the folly of some of the presuppositions that homosexual proponents and activists raise in support of the normality of homosexuality. I found his discussion of the dangers of thinking that homosexuality is an innocuous and legitimate alternative lifestyle, and of what he called the "cultural creeds" that led us to our current destination, to be very insightful. In the last section of the book Pastor Christopher provides a very helpful strategy for the church as we face the onslaught of an unbiblical and destructive perspective on marriage and sexuality. After examining Scripture and the strongest arguments of those who say that same-sex marriage is really the same as traditional marriage, the author cogently and convincingly demonstrates that the answer to the question in the title of the book is "no, they are not the same."

Dr. Wayne Mack, biblical counselor, lecturer, and author of numerous books related to biblical counseling

Commendations

The issue of same-sex marriage is currently much debated in South Africa. This is partly due to new laws and the differences of opinion between various churches and denominations. The advocates of same-sex marriage are very vocal, often making use of so-called "scientific facts." This book by Mark Christopher gives a new perspective from the other side in an accountable way. Its publication must be welcomed by all asking for a biblical perspective on such a contentious issue.

Prof. H. F. van Rooy, Professor of Old Testament, North-West University, Potchefstroom, South Africa

This is a brief but compelling examination of "same-sex marriage"—politely called "civil partnership" in the United Kingdom—from a biblical perspective. It is clear, cogent, and written in a good spirit. While being informative itself, it has a most valuable bibliography, which makes it useful for those who wish to pursue the subject further.

Paul E. Brown, editor, Homosexuality: Christian Truth and Love, UK

To Pastor and Mrs. Stange,

whose love, godly example, and patient guidance

never failed to point me in the direction of the cross!

"Marriage is to be held in honor among all,
and the marriage bed is to be undefiled;
for fornicators and adulterers God will judge."
Hebrews 13:4

Contents

A note to the reader

What began as a seminar at the 2005 South African Shepherd's Conference has now blossomed into a more detailed book on a most sensitive and difficult subject: same-sex marriage (SSM), or "civil unions," as they are known in many European countries.[1]

Since that seminar, many have encouraged me to put the proverbial pen to paper. To those who encouraged me—Thanks! Your persistence and prayers have motivated me to write what follows.

Given the fact that there are already a number of good books on the subject of SSM (these are listed in the Bibliography), I decided to write a summary of some key thoughts and arguments that I hope will be helpful to those who are struggling with the issue. Now that many countries have legalized SSM or civil unions, this book is all the more relevant. For all those in churches and denominations that have conceded very valuable terrain on this issue, this book is for you. It is aimed at all those who don't have the time or inclination to read a more thorough book on the subject.

Because this is a brief treatise on what is otherwise a very involved topic, I am sure there will be those who will be disappointed in the concise treatment of certain points, or even in the complete omission of some aspects of the debate. Brevity does not always lend itself to clarity. The concise nature of the book has, in fact, been the biggest challenge. I hope I have not sacrificed clarity and understanding on the altar of brevity.

For those whose interest is piqued for a more thorough handling of the subject matter, please consult the Bibliography and look for the citations that have an asterisk—those are the works I highly recommend.

What is written here is meant to point to redemption in Jesus Christ, not rancor at the gay community. I realize that not all in the gay community are in agreement with some of the activists I cite. The fact remains, however, that there are some very troubling moral trends emerging from many of the gay-rights advocates that need to be exposed. Yet this does not give the church license to engage in this battle in an unloving or uncharitable way. For this reason, I ardently admonish the church. The church has much of which to repent where marriage and family issues are concerned. We must clean our own house first if we wish to turn the tide on the troubling trends highlighted in this book.

A special thanks to Jim Holmes of Day One Publications and my editor,

Suzanne Mitchell, who both patiently guided me along the publication trail while making many needful and valuable suggestions along the way!

Finally, to my dear wife, Debbie, and to my children, Janelle and Micaiah, thanks for unselfishly allowing me the time needed to research and write this. I promise to make it up to you!

"Now to Him who is able to do far more abundantly beyond all that we ask or think, according to the power that works within us, to Him be the glory in the church and in Christ Jesus to all generations forever and ever. Amen" (Eph. 3:20–21).

Notes

1 Civil unions or civil partnerships differ from same-sex marriage in that they grant the relationship the legal, state, and fiscal benefits of marriage without the full recognition of marriage. This approach is a compromise on the part of many governments in order to try to appease both sides of this very contentious issue. Some church leaders see this as a satisfactory compromise. I contend that civil unions still demean marriage as many heterosexual couples will opt for such arrangements to avoid the "religious" aspects of marriage. In the end, many SSM advocates are not entirely satisfied with civil unions because they say that such unions still stop short of marriage and are, therefore, discriminatory.

Introduction

Realizing the unthinkable

It was Francis Schaeffer who commented that "People drift along from generation to generation, and the morally unthinkable becomes thinkable as the years move on."[1] From our current cultural vantage point, Schaeffer's comment is as prophetic as it is insightful!

Because the unthinkable has now become thinkable, I feel a lot like the airline pilot who, upon reaching cruising altitude, announced to his passengers that he had both good news and bad news. He continued, "The bad news is that we have drifted way off course. The good news is that we are making excellent time." The issue of same-sex marriage (SSM) is no different. Recent legislation regarding SSM in South Africa, for example, highlights just how far off course we are as a society. What is so sad is that we have arrived at this destination rather rapidly.

So how should the church of Jesus Christ respond to this twenty-first-century moral and spiritual crossroads of SSM? Only twenty years ago, such a possibility seemed remote indeed. But now, in many Western societies, we are facing laws of the land that legalize SSM. How did we arrive at this destination? As two gay activists, Marshall Kirk and Hunter Marsden, declare, "Almost any behavior begins to look normal if you are exposed to enough of it."[2] Hence, the concerted onslaught of the mainstream media, hedonistic Hollywood, liberal scholars, radical activists, a compliant judiciary, and pragmatic politicians have all blitzkrieged our senses to make the unthinkable thinkable.

Now that SSM is the law *de jure* in many countries, what can we, the church, expect? What influences are behind the SSM lobby? Further, how should we as the church respond? What follows is meant to answer these questions. This work is a concise, penetrating analysis of the plight SSM and gay rights pose to marriage, family, and the Bible-believing church at large. This exposé seeks not only to inform the church in recognizing the moral dangers and logical outcomes of SSM, but also to prescribe some corrective measures to curb the moral slippage that has helped contribute to this plight in the first place.

Framing the debate: four nonnegotiables

Before proceeding any further, I would like to make four caveats that will serve to frame what follows:

First, this argument is not about hate but debate. It has become commonplace for SSM advocates to cry pejoratively "homophobe," "fundamentalist," and "homophobia" every time someone disagrees with them. As Katherine Young and Paul Nathanson, an avowed homosexual scholar who is opposed to SSM, contend,

> This argument amounts to verbal terrorism. By "homophobic" is meant prejudice and hostility, although this word actually connotes the neuroticism of a phobia. The implication is that only evil or sick people can possibly disagree with any claim made by gay people. (Never mind that not even all gay people are in favor of gay marriage.) Moreover, this is an *ad hominem* [appealing to the emotions] argument. It is easy to trivialize arguments by attacking the personal integrity of those who make them. That way, you need not deal with the argument itself.[3]

With that in mind, it is simply my goal to speak the truth in love and to interact with the arguments of the topic rather than attack people. My interest here is not to resort to verbal volleys and name-calling, but to deal biblically and honestly with the substance of the arguments.[4]

Second, it must always be remembered that, in the Bible, homosexuality isn't necessarily worse than other sexual sins. The Bible often lumps a variety of sexual sins together, such as fornication, immorality, adultery, and incest. In the end, it takes no more grace for God to save a homosexual than it does to save an adulterer or fornicator. The cross of Christ always provides a level playing field!

The question might be asked, "Then why single out homosexuality and SSM?" The answer to this is quite simple: because this particular vice is being vigorously promoted, placarded, and politicized. I do not know of any organized attempts to legitimize adultery, incest, or the like.

Third, I concede right up front that my authority is the Bible, the Word of God. For this reason, much of what I say is based on my knowledge of Scripture even when I don't quote from it directly. Much of the debate swirling around this issue goes back to the authority of the first three chapters of the Bible, Genesis 1 through 3. Even pro-gay theologians like Richard Whitaker recognize this:

There is no question that the creation accounts of Genesis 1–3 (specifically, in Gen. 1:26–27 and 2:24) are fundamental to the discussion about homosexuality in the church. Most scholars agree that these texts are critical, even though they contain no clear reference to homosexuality. It is important to pay close attention to the larger context of these narratives, that is, Genesis 1–3 ...[5]

Therefore, much of what I say must be filtered through the penetrating lens of Genesis 1–3.

Finally, because pro-gay theologians are often vague about the "God" they worship, it is imperative for me to state briefly who the biblical God is. In short, the God I refer to is the Sovereign Creator of the universe (Isa. 40:1–31). He is personal and involved with his creation, while simultaneously remaining independent of it (Isa. 55:8–9). For this reason God is not bound by, nor contained in, his creation. He is a holy, immutable (changeless) Spirit being who cannot be confined in the futile imagination of man (Lev. 11:44; Mal. 3:6; John 4:24). He can only be revealed as he is in his Word.

My church's opening statement of faith under the doctrine of God summarizes well the God I reference throughout these pages: "We teach that there is but one living and true God (Deuteronomy 6:4; Isaiah 45:5–7; 1 Corinthians 8:4), an infinite, all-knowing Spirit (John 4:24), perfect in all His attributes, one in essence, eternally existing in three persons—Father, Son, and Holy Spirit (Matthew 28:19; 2 Corinthians 13:14)—each equally deserving worship and obedience."[6]

This view of God is critical when approaching a significant moral issue like homosexuality and SSM. A person's view of the Bible and of God will ultimately determine where he or she lands on this vital issue. As A. W. Tozer so insightfully noted in his wonderful book *The Knowledge of the Holy*,

The history of mankind will probably show that no people has ever risen above its religion, and man's spiritual history will positively demonstrate that no religion has ever been greater than its idea of God. Worship is pure or base as the worshiper entertains high or low thoughts of God … Always the most revealing thing about the Church is her idea of God, just as her most significant message is what she says about Him or leaves unsaid, for her silence is often more eloquent than her speech …7

A high view of God, like the one advocated in this book, insists that God's moral standards directly correspond to his unimpeachable character. His holy standards are as unchangeable as his immutable nature. Therefore, man does not have the right to decide arbitrarily what marriage is or is not, nor does he have the right to alter God's holy proscriptions (prohibitions) regarding sexuality. Divorced from a high view of God, the church and society at large launch forth into a morally ambiguous world—amorality. So I reject the pantheistic (God is all and all is God) and neo-gnostic, man-centered permutations of God that are often implied by the proponents of SSM.[8]

The vastness of the topic of SSM is such that I can only briefly survey the issue and critique it as we go along. So, for the purposes of this work, I will endeavor to answer six critical questions about SSM:

- What is the purpose of marriage? This is fundamental in understanding God's stated intention for the divine institution of marriage. The big question here is: Has God's purpose for marriage changed?
- What presuppositions motivate the SSM lobby? Here we will quickly see that SSM is not really the ultimate goal, but rather a means to an agenda-driven end.
- What are some of the key dangers of legalized SSM? I have often been asked, "Why don't we just give gays SSM? Then maybe they will leave us alone." Such an attitude exhibits a level of naiveté that is more closely aligned with wishful thinking than reality.
- How did we get here? It is helpful to mention some of the popular streams of thought that have helped create an atmosphere that is conducive for legalizing SSM.
- How should the church (the true church of actual believers) respond to SSM? Without a doubt, the church at large has, more often than not, been a part of the problem rather than the solution. We now need

a basic battle plan for countering the ravages of the SSM onslaught. How should we proceed?

- Can homosexuals change? It is often dogmatically asserted that homosexuals are born with a homosexual "orientation," and that, therefore, the homosexual lifestyle is as inevitable as it is immutable. But what does the Bible say?

Notes

1 **C. Everett Koop** and **Francis Schaeffer,** *Whatever Happened to the Human Race?* (Wheaton, IL: Crossway, 1983), p. 2.

2 Quoted in **Erwin Lutzer,** *The Truth about Same-Sex Marriage: 6 Things You Need to Know about What's Really at Stake* (Chicago: Moody Press, 2004), p. 13.

3 **Katherine K. Young** and **Paul Nathanson,** "Marriage à la Mode: Answering Advocates of Gay Marriage," 2003, at marriageinstitute.ca, p. 10.

4 Much of the pro-gay literature I have read (and I have read much) tends to favor *ad hominem* arguments that tar all who disagree with the pro-gay position. This type of logic fails to deal adequately with the substance of the issue. This is why *ad hominem* attacks are often a tacit admission of faulty arguments that subjectively refuse to consider the other side of the debate.

5 **Richard Whitaker,** "Creation and Human Sexuality," in **Choon-Leong Seow,** ed., *Homosexuality and Christian Community* (Louisville, KY: Westminster John Knox Press, 1996), p. 3.

6 Statement of Faith, Living Hope Bible Church, Wynberg, South Africa, 2003, p. 1.

7 **A. W. Tozer,** *The Knowledge of the Holy* (San Francisco: Harper & Row, 1978), p. 9.

8 Author and scholar **Peter Jones** has addressed the New Age tendencies of pro-gay theologians in his excellent books *Pagans in the Pews* and *The God of Sex* (see the Bibliography).

1. What is the divine purpose for marriage?

The answer to this question depends on the person to whom one talks. But, from a Christian perspective, this question is best answered by surveying the basic elements of marriage as presented in Genesis 1 and 2. God's original blueprint for marriage sets the stage for discovering God's wonderful purpose and plan for marriage. As the saying goes, "When in doubt, consult the owner's manual!" Sadly, SSM advocates question the authority and veracity of the Bible. This is the only way they can reason the way they do. I have often wondered why they even bother with the Bible at all. Yet they are oddly constrained to seek validation for the sin of homosexuality from the Word of God in an effort to marginalize and try to blunt its influence on this issue. One could rightly ask why SSM advocates are not as aggressive in their attempts to harmonize SSM and homosexuality with other religious writings, such as the Koran!

It is of extreme importance that the debate is properly framed from God's Word. It is hardly an accident that the first three chapters of the Bible directly address the issue of marriage, which was God's first ordained institution. It is in the first two chapters of Genesis that we find a number of foundational elements concerning gender distinction, marriage, and sexuality that are instructive for our understanding of what marriage is from God's perspective.

Marriage is reflective

According to Genesis 1:26–27,

Then God said, "Let Us make man in Our *image*, according to Our *likeness*; and let them rule over the fish of the sea and over the birds of the sky and over the cattle and over all the earth, and over every creeping thing that creeps on the earth." God created man in His own *image*, in the image of God He created him; male and female He created them [emphasis added].

The ultimate purpose of marriage is seen in that marriage reflects God and his image.[1] This is not to imply that singles don't represent the image of God. Both genders reflect the *imago dei* (image of God) in very different and yet complementary ways. The male and female are distinct and unique, but, when united in a covenant commitment before God and then brought together in physical intimacy, they mirror essential aspects of the triune Godhead in a way the rest of creation never can or will! Gender distinction is a creational reality, not a result of social or cultural constructs.[2] This is one of the reasons why God does not endorse transsexuality, transvestism, and transgenderism. Gender-bending is antithetical to the unique distinctions God implanted in the man and woman from the dawn of creation.

Any attempt to androgynize (merge or blend together) men and women, as both the feminist and homosexual lobbies have done, is tantamount to defacing God. The androgynous ideal seeks to erase the gender distinctions God intended from creation. SSM, whether intentionally or unintentionally, insists on giving God an extreme makeover he neither wants nor needs. For this reason, this issue is as much about gender distinction as it is about sex and sexuality.

Marriage is meant to be completion

Genesis 2:18 says, "Then the LORD God said, 'It is not good for the man to be alone; I will make him a helper suitable for him.'"

It was not "good" (not beneficial or fitting) for Adam to be alone, so God created a "helper." Eve was the missing ingredient of this creational ordinance. As a helper, Eve made up that which was lacking in Adam. This was something the rest of creation was unable to do, because the rest of creation was and is devoid of image-bearing qualities. Though Eve was very different from Adam, she was still very much like him. In this way, Eve was the perfect corresponding opposite, or complement, to Adam! Had God made them exactly alike, Eve could not have provided the necessary attributes to complement and so complete Adam.

It is never good for man to be alone. The fulfilled life is found only in community with other image-bearers. This, in part, is what it means to be an image-bearer. This is why the chimps and other primates at your local zoo or circus can never fill the social void of humanity. Yet male and female together, in a covenant oath before God, find completion and fulfillment.

The point is simple: men and women are different and yet similar at the same time. The result of this contrasted correspondence is completion. SSM seeks to ignore the differences and redefine the completion. Yet one has to overlook the obvious to achieve this level of denial. Think of all the biological differences between the sexes. Last time I checked, only women could gestate and lactate! Then, on the emotional front, think of the many dissimilarities. For example:[3]

- Men are often more physically aggressive, while women are sometimes more sensitive and understanding. This is why most of the spousal abuse that takes place in marriages is perpetrated by men.
- Men often find analytical thought easier, while women are often more intuitive.
- Men are more contemplative, while women are more communicative. Two of the commonest complaints from couples I have counseled over the years is that "he doesn't communicate," while "she talks too much."
- Men respond sexually more by sight; while women respond more to emotional connections. In all of the adultery cases in which I have counseled, the affairs began with flirtatious advances and strong emotional connections. The men confide they were physically attracted to the other women; while the women admit to an attraction based on an emotional appeal that developed over time.
- Men require immediate justice, while women are more inclined to compassion. This is, in part, why it is often heard that women should rule the world instead of men, because it is thought that women would not be as quick to go to war.

Just think how valuable these distinctions are in child-rearing! Both sides of the equation are crucial ingredients in the enterprise of parenting. When temperately demonstrated and modeled before children in the home, these contrasting characteristics can help produce healthier and better-adjusted children.[4] Sadly, same-sex couples will never be able to offer these much-needed gender differences to any children they might have.[5]

This is precisely why men and women complement each other so well. It is by divine design! Adam and Eve were a perfect, corresponding pair. They corresponded physically, mentally, emotionally, socially, and spiritually. Glenn Stanton and Dr. Bill Maier, the authors of *Marriage on Trial*, write,

Marriages don't bring similar things together. They bring different things together and help them work for a common good. Same-sex unions are not marriage because they don't bring the two different parts of humanity together. They bring similar things together, thus the word same in "same-sex marriage" ... Women complete men, and men complete women ... A man can't complete another man, nor can a woman complete another woman.[6]

They go on to make the crucial point that SSM ultimately robs a family of true dignity: "Same-sex families seeking equality with the natural family devalue humanity because they proclaim that one part of humanity is unnecessary. Women help men become what they are created to be, and men help women become what they were created to be. To deny this is to deny our full, God-given humanity."[7]

Therefore, SSM is not complementary. Rather it seeks to bypass God's requirement of making up that which is lacking in one's spouse. Perhaps this is one of the reasons why homosexuals often have such a difficult time with committed, monogamous relationships.[8]

Marriage is meant to be cohesive
Genesis 2:22–24 says,

The LORD God fashioned into a woman the rib which He had taken from the man, and brought her to the man. The man said,

"This is now bone of my bones,
And flesh of my flesh;
She shall be called Woman,
Because she was taken out of Man."

For this reason a man shall leave his father and his mother, and shall be joined [cleave] to his wife; and they shall become one flesh.

The "oneness" in verse 24 is a uni-plurality, which is the glue that serves to merge together the distinctions of Adam and Eve into one cohesive unit. The conscious act of the joining together, or cleaving, leads to the emphasized result of "one flesh," where two are now made into one. The term used for "one" (*echad*) is the same term used to describe the unity of God in Deuteronomy 6:4, where Israel's God is said to be "one." This active cleaving is the glue that binds the two corresponding parts together into an indissoluble whole. This implies three interrelated aspects of marriage:

1. This "oneness" speaks of *companionship*. This is closely related to the marriage element of cohesiveness; marriage unites two opposites into a unit that produces a distinctive level of companionship that could never be achieved in an SSM.

2. This "oneness" also speaks of *commitment*. This commitment is expressed in a mutual, unconditional covenant before God and each other as witnessed by our fellow man (see Gen. 2:23). Then, and only then, comes the physical bond of intimacy. This intimate act forms a physical, emotional, mental, volitional, and spiritual bond that is exceedingly strong because it involves the total person. In 1 Corinthians, the apostle Paul underscores this same idea:

Or do you not know that the one who joins himself to a prostitute is one body *with her*? For He says, "The two shall become one flesh." But the one who joins himself to the Lord is one spirit *with Him*. Flee immorality. Every *other* sin that a man commits is outside the body, but the immoral man sins against his own body. (1 Cor. 6:16–18, emphasis added)

Paul's argument is that sexual sin of any nature is different from other sins because it involves the whole person, body, mind, and spirit. The consequences of violating God's standards here affect every facet of one's being. Sexual sin of any kind is unique among all other sin in that it acts like a stain to the soul. This is why sexual abuse, rape, incest, and adultery are so hard to overcome, because the whole person has been violated and these acts are devoid of the commitment intended from the beginning. Erwin Lutzer explains, "The sexual bond can be so powerful that it can even determine the direction of a person's orientation."[9]

For this reason, among others, God's sequential recipe for marriage is: one man and one woman in a covenant commitment that subsequently expresses itself in sexual union, which, in part, symbolizes the union of body, mind, and spirit! This is why physical intimacy apart from the covenant commitment cannot equal marriage and is not considered marriage in God's sight (Mal. 2:14; John 4:17–18). Such extra-marital relationships form an alien bond and stain the soul, but they don't equal marriage. So it is no coincidence that, historically, every successful culture and society has maintained matrimonial rituals and social celebrations of affirmation. Such indicate the approval for the wedded couple now to live together as one.

3. Further, this "oneness" speaks of *permanence*—also known as monogamy. Marriage is a bond of unity that should not be broken except by death. Ephesians 5:22–33 clearly records that Christ cannot be severed from his bride, the church. Can the unity of the trinity (tri-unity) be severed? Yet SSM unions are seemingly incapable of monogamy. According to the research of Dr. Timothy J. Daily on the issue of monogamy among homosexuals,

While the rate of fidelity within marriage (heterosexual) cited by these studies remains far from ideal, there is a significant difference between the negligible lifetime fidelity rate for homosexuals and the 75 to 90 percent for married couples. This indicates that even "committed" homosexual relationships display a fundamental incapacity for the faithfulness and commitment that is axiomatic to the institution of marriage.[10]

Dr. Daily concludes that monogamy in the gay community is not possible because homosexuals see sexual relationships "primarily for pleasure," and they are taught, thanks to the sexual revolution, that "monogamy in marriage is not the norm."[11]

Now, contrast this with heterosexual marriages, in which 75 per cent of married partners are faithful to their vows in the first ten years of marriage.

Additionally, of those heterosexuals who do get divorced, many do so after ten years of marriage. Interestingly, one seventy-year longitudinal study found that divorce takes six years off each of the affected spouses' lives and four years off the lives of each of their children.[12] As a side note, smoking takes six years off a smoker's life. Perhaps, just as smokers sue the tobacco companies for the consequences of smoking, so victims of divorce should sue their governments and judicial systems for making divorce so easy. Yet one local SSM advocate, when making his case for SSM in the South African paper *The Cape Times*, wrote,

In the case of lesbian and gay couples, they commit to honour, respect, support, and love each other. Such covenants are intended to be exclusive and permanent, the basis of creating a new family model that will not only have the stability necessary to rear children (if the couple wishes to do so) but will also sustain the partners to the end of their lives.[13]

Such specious thinking does not intersect with reality. All the statistics I've seen indicate a blatant incongruity between the homosexual lifestyle and monogamy.[14] In short,

… homosexuality is against nature. The plumbing doesn't work. We weren't designed this way. When homosexuals ignore nature, first they invite into their own bodies all sorts of infectious diseases. Second, there are emotional problems. Even in every homosexual relationship, there is a male and female role. One of them plays the male or the dominant partner, and the other plays the female. This shows by nature God has made us male and female. He has made each sex to complement each other.[15]

In the same vein, Dr. Camille Paglia, a lesbian scholar and author, categorically states,

Homosexuality is not normal. On the contrary it is a challenge to the norm … Nature exists whether academics like it or not. And in nature, procreation is the single relentless rule. That is the norm. Our sexual bodies were designed for reproduction … No one is born gay. The idea is ridiculous … Homosexuality is an adaptation, not an inborn trait.[16]

What a refreshingly honest admission from the other side of the debate!

John Piper offers a nice summary of this cohesive principle: "By creating a person *like* Adam yet very *unlike* Adam, God provided the possibility of a profound unity that would otherwise have been impossible. There is a different kind of unity enjoyed by the joining of diverse counterparts than is enjoyed by joining two things just alike … So God made a woman and not a man. He created heterosexuality, not homosexuality. God's first institution was marriage, not the fraternity."[17]

Marriage is meant to be productive

Genesis 1:28 says, "God blessed them; and God said to them, 'Be fruitful and multiply, and fill the earth, and subdue it; and rule over the fish of the sea and over the birds of the sky and over every living thing that moves on the earth.'"

Now, granted, procreation is not the only reason for marriage, but it certainly is a very good reason. Mankind is meant to propagate and to perpetuate this unique and dynamic image-bearing species. It doesn't take a Rhodes Scholar to figure out the obvious fact that it takes a man and a woman to procreate naturally. Consider that males have both X and Y chromosomes, while females have only pairs of X chromosomes. It is the presence of the Y chromosome that determines whether the baby is a boy or a girl. Whether feminists like it or not, the man's chromosomes determine the gender of the baby.

In a recent constitutional court battle in South Africa over SSM, one of the advocates for SSM indicated that the focus on procreation in marriage had become socially and technologically obsolete: "Procreation is not a defining characteristic of conjugal relations. This would be doubly offensive to those couples who are not able to procreate."[18]

SSM proponents try to divorce sexuality from its procreative aspects. But, left to themselves, homosexuals would soon die out. Evolutionists call this the "survival of the fittest." The presupposition behind SSM thinking is the notion that sexuality is a purely biological response for self-gratification. Yet, as one informed journalist in *World Magazine* reminds us,

Marriage is not just about love or sex or companionship. It is about establishing a nuclear family. Marriage is not for everybody ... Nevertheless, what marriage does is establish a new family. And families are the bricks of which every society, every culture, every government is built ... Families form clans, clans form tribes, and eventually tribes come together in nations ... When the family falls apart, so does the nation and so does the culture.[19]

It must be remembered that, as part of the creation mandate, God created Adam and Eve to serve as his representatives and caretakers of creation. As image-bearing creatures, they were meant to subdue and rule the earth. Apart from procreation, this dominion capacity could never be realized. This is why God repeated the command to procreate after the global flood (Gen. 9:1–7).

Marriage is meant to be exhilarating
See Genesis 2:23. Proverbs 5:18–19 declares,

Let your fountain be blessed,
And rejoice in the wife of your youth.
As a loving hind and a graceful doe,
Let her breasts satisfy you at all times;
Be exhilarated always with her love.

God is not a cosmic prude who disapproves of sexual relations. To oppose immorality is not the same as opposing sex. Yet promoters of SSM take great delight in trying to portray the biblical view of sex as anything but pleasurable. In fact, God not only encourages a healthy and vibrant sex life, he also commands it (1 Cor. 7:3–7)! But God's proviso is that sex should remain within *his established boundaries* of a heterosexual, covenant commitment. Marriage regulates our sexual activity and desires. Without marriage, you have the mess spawned by the sexual revolution— unwed mothers, illegitimate children, fatherless homes, shattered emotions, ruined relationships, and unchecked desires.

In summary, the heterosexual norm of marriage provides many necessary benefits to both individuals and society at large![20] This Genesis creational schematic is consistently maintained throughout the Bible. God never amends it nor appends anything to it. Christ himself reaffirmed it, as did the apostle Paul:

Some Pharisees came to Jesus, testing Him and asking, "Is it lawful for a man to divorce his wife for any reason at all?" And He answered and said, "Have you not read that He who created them from the beginning made them male and female, and said, 'For this reason a man shall leave his father and mother and be joined to his wife, and the two shall become one flesh'? So they are no longer two, but one flesh. What therefore God has joined together, let no man separate." (Matt. 19:3–6)

So husbands ought also to love their own wives as their own bodies. He who loves his own wife loves himself; for no one ever hated his own flesh, but nourishes and cherishes it, just as Christ also does the church, because we are members of His body. "For this reason a man shall leave his father and mother and shall be joined to his wife, and the two shall become one flesh." This mystery is great; but I am speaking with reference to Christ and the church. (Eph. 5:28–32)[21]

Even though Christ never specifically addressed homosexuality, he said all that needed to be said about marriage and sexuality when he reaffirmed the Genesis 2 creational mandate! He didn't address pedophilia, bestiality, or necrophilia either, but he didn't need to as he underscored and reaffirmed the Genesis 2 ideal for marriage.

It must be concluded that marriage has a multifaceted meaning attached to it from the moment of creation. It is as complex as it is unalterable. To modify it arbitrarily to accommodate one's sin is to invite the judgment of God.[22] The New Testament clearly reaffirms the Genesis creation mandate for marriage. God has never altered his plan, even in light of the Fall in Genesis 3.

It is clear from the biblical account of marriage that it is a divine institution, not a mere civil arrangement. As such, civil government can only recognize what God has clearly ordained.

Notes

1 This is not to imply that some physical representation is inherent in the idea of the image of God in man, for God is Spirit. Rather, what is meant by the image of God in man has more to do with those divinely communicated factors that enable man to fulfill the mandate of dominion over creation. Humanity serves as God's representative over all of creation. For this reason, man bears the image of God. This is what uniquely distinguishes us from the rest of creation. Hence we can effectively communicate, plan, work, and socialize in ways the rest of creation cannot. Our dignity stems from our image-bearing qualities!

2 It is often maintained by pro-gay activists that the traditional understanding of the male/female distinction is a result of a "heteropatriarchal" understanding of the Bible. There are many gays and feminists who see gender distinctions, biological and otherwise, as a result of social constructs. Therefore, they surmise, if we can rid ourselves of the traditional understanding by adopting a new social construct, then society will be free to see that there aren't really any differences between the sexes. Then true equality will be achieved. This is the same thinking that has fueled the promotion of gender-free restrooms at many colleges and universities in the USA.

3 These five examples are not meant to stereotype either sex. I realize these are not absolute, but just pastoral observations with a measure of truth behind them. I do understand that these are not as true as they once were because of the feminist movement and more women in the workplace. Some of these mindsets are changing as men become more feminized and women become more masculinized. Researchers **Dr. Bill Maier** and **Glenn T. Stanton** address this issue of the differing emotional makeup of the sexes in Chapter 10 of their excellent book *Marriage on Trial: The Case against Same-Sex Marriage and Parenting* (Downers Grove, IL: IVP, 2004), pp. 113–120). Also see **Greg Johnson,** "The Biological Basis for Gender-Specific Behavior," in **John Piper** and **Wayne Grudem,** eds., *Recovering Biblical Manhood & Womanhood: A Response to Evangelical Feminism* (Wheaton, IL: Crossway, 1991), pp. 280–293.

4 Think of the little boy who falls off his bicycle and hurts himself while breaking his bike at the same time. To whom does the boy run for comfort and healing? Mom, of course. But when it is time to fix the bike, to whom does he run then? Dad! Both a mom and a dad are needed when raising a child. This helps produce a well-rounded and fulfilled individual. In light of the breakdown of the family in the West, it is no wonder so many suffer from identity crises and emotional distress.

5 A recent secular article indicates the importance and distinction of the father's role in parenting: "Dad's Love is Different from Mom's Love," March 20, 2007, capetimes.co.za/index.php?fSectionId=3531&fArticleId=iol1174302585241F364.

6 **Dr. Bill Maier** and **Glenn T. Stanton,** *Marriage on Trial: The Case against Same-Sex Marriage and Parenting* (Downers Grove, IL: IVP, 2004), p. 126.

7 Ibid. p. 173.

8 Authors **David P. McWhirter** and **Andrew M. Mattison** studied 156 homosexual relationships lasting from one to thirty-seven years. They concluded that "Only seven couples have a totally exclusive sexual relationship, and these men all have been together for less than five years. Stated another way, all couples with a lasting relationship lasting more than five years have incorporated some provision for outside sexual activity in their relationships." *The Male Couple: How Relationships Develop* (Englewood Cliffs, NJ: Prentice-Hall, 1984), pp. 252–253.

9 **Erwin W. Lutzer,** *The Truth about Same-Sex Marriage: 6 Things You Need to Know about What's Really at Stake* (Chicago: Moody Press, 2004), p. 54.

10 Daily's article is filled with citations from a number of studies that have been done on this issue of gay monogamy. It makes for very worthwhile reading. **Timothy J. Daily, Ph.D.,** "Comparing the Lifestyle of Homosexual Couples to Married Couples," p. 6, at frc.org.

11 Ibid. p. 6.

12 **Kathleen M. Clark et al,** "A Longitudinal Study of Religiosity and Mortality Risk," *Journal of Health Psychology,* 4:3 (1999), pp. 381–391.

13 **Pieter Oberholzer,** "Gay Couples' Covenants with Each Other and God Exist, Regardless of Church Attitude," *The Cape Times*, August 17, 2004, p. 9.

14 One study concluded that, of the gay men surveyed, 60% had at least 250 sexual partners; 28% had more than 1,000 sexual partners. Of those surveyed, 79% admitted that more than half their partners were total strangers! **Joseph P. Gudal,** "Homosexuality: Fact and Fiction," Christian Research Institute, at equip.org. Also see Daily, "Comparing the Lifestyle," who corroborates these findings and provides a number of other, more recent studies that closely approximate these statistical findings.

15 **D. James Kennedy** and **Jerry Newcomb,** *What's Wrong with Same-Sex Marriage?* (Wheaton, IL: Crossway, 2004), p. 55.

16 Quoted in **Maier** and **Stanton,** *Marriage on Trial*, p. 138.

17 **John Piper,** "Marriage: A Matrix of Christian Hedonism," October 16, 1983, at desiringgod.org.

18 **Jenni Evans,** "Constitutional Court Battle over Gay Marriage Begins," *The Cape Times*, May 18, 2005.

19 The Editors, "Nuclear Fission," August 9, 2003, at world.mag.com.

20 Maier and **Stanton,** *Marriage on Trial*, p. 129.

21 The Ephesians 5:22–32 passage illustrates what marriage symbolizes: the relationship of Christ as head over his bride, the church! Any form of marriage other than that promoted in Genesis 1 and 2 fails to illustrate this most crucial relationship between Christ and the church. God mandated the marriage blueprint to concretely mirror the relationship that Christ would ultimately have with his bride. SSM fails to reflect the Ephesians 5:22–32 ideal, because it erases the vital distinctions God intended.

22 Genesis 6:1–4 recounts some base manner of perversion regarding the Genesis 1 and 2 institution of marriage. The net result was the universal flood. To abandon God's plan for marriage by thinking we can somehow improve upon it is to abandon God. Romans 1:18–32 makes it clear that God gives individuals and societies over to their perversions when they reject him and his commands (Rom. 1:24, 26, 28). It is of extreme significance that Matthew 24:36–38 and Luke 17:28–29 declare that the timing of Jesus's second coming will parallel the same basic conditions which existed during the flood and Sodom and Gomorrah judgments, respectively. Could it be that a gross perversion of the Genesis creation ordinance of marriage will be one of the defining features of Christ's second coming?

2. What presuppositions motivate the SSM lobby?

Presupposition 1: Genetic orientation. Is it in the genes?

Without a doubt, the principal SSM presupposition is that of "orientation." The claim of "orientation" is, in large measure, that it is an inborn genetic trait that is as absolute as it is unalterable. At least, this is the governing assumption. The argument goes something like this: "If you are born that way, then it can't be helped, and you bear absolutely no responsibility for your actions." So any notions to the contrary are deemed to be unscientific discrimination against this biologically constituted state. After all, being born a homosexual is just like being born with brown hair, blue eyes, or white skin, isn't it?

Once it is assumed and accepted that homosexuality is a biologically constituted state, then it logically follows that homosexuals must be accorded the same civil rights as racial minorities or those who are afflicted with disability. Yet, as we will see, homosexuality is, unlike race and disability, neither involuntary nor immutable.

If the orientation argument is true, what about rapists and pedophiles, to use two examples? Perhaps they too are biologically consigned to such behavior. So we shouldn't be so quick to judge them, as they were born that way. Instead, maybe we should be more tolerant and seek to understand them, and even protect their right to follow their genetic inclinations. Once they achieve true equality, perhaps they won't pose such a threat to society.[1]

In this whole debate we must distinguish between biological influences and biological determinism. It is entirely possible for a person to have certain predispositions (a mindset) that may incline him or her to certain activities such as alcoholism or homosexuality. But to be *inclined* is not the same as being *consigned* toward certain behaviors. It is a far cry from biological determinism. In spite of such influences, change is still possible, and, with a measure of self-control and proactive planning, a person can be kept from falling into the trap to begin with.

One example of the strained lengths to which SSM advocates will go is seen in the pseudo-science offered as proof of a pre-existing biological condition. One such study that was hailed by the news media as "proof" that homosexuality is biologically determined was carried out by Dr. Simon Levay, a neuroscientist from the Salk Institute for Biological Studies in San Diego.

Dr. Levay studied the hypothalamus gland in the human brain, which supposedly determines sexual orientation. He studied forty-one brains from cadavers which included nineteen homosexual men. In each of those gay men, the hypothalamus gland was less than half the size found in their heterosexual counterparts. This was hailed by the gay community and mainstream media as irrefutable evidence that homosexuals are born that way. But as Dr. John Money from John Hopkins University and Medical Center cautioned, "Of course it, sexual orientation, is in the brain. The real question is when did it get there? Was it prenatal, neonatal, during childhood or puberty? That we don't know."[2]

Not surprisingly, there were a number of serious flaws with Dr. Levay's findings:

- All nineteen homosexual men died of AIDS, which many researchers believe contributed to the difference in the size of the hypothalamus.
- The sexual history of all the test subjects was completely unknown, which leaves many unanswered questions concerning the test subjects and, ultimately, the conclusions of the study. The other men were presumed to have been heterosexual, but could any of them have been bisexual or even gay at one time?
- It must be asked whether the smaller hypothalamus glands were the cause or the result of homosexual activity. The mainstream press assumes that the smaller hypothalamus glands are the predicative catalyst that determines one's sexual orientation. No one has thought to probe any further by asking the logical questions.
- Dr. Levay's study has never been successfully replicated, even by him! For something to be deemed scientific, it must be repeatable, especially by other scientists.
- Dr. Levay was a practicing homosexual who lost a lover to AIDS. It

would appear that this jaundiced his objectivity so that he was not entirely dispassionate in his scientific pursuit.

- Finally, Dr. Levay himself admitted, "It's important to stress what I didn't find. I did not prove that homosexuality was genetic, or find a genetic cause for being gay. I didn't show that gay men are born that way, the most common mistake people make in interpreting my work."[3]

In another landmark study that has been hailed as more proof that genetics play a huge role in determining homosexuality, psychologist Michael Bailey of Northwestern University and psychiatrist Richard Pillard of Boston University School of Medicine (who is gay) researched pairs of identical (monozygotic) twins. Their findings revealed that in half the instances where one of the twins was homosexual, the other one was as well. This was hailed as proof of a "gay" gene.[4]

Yet this study was also riddled with anomalies. For instance:

- Identical twins have exactly the same genes, so for this gene theory to prove true, you would expect a 100 per cent concordance (correspondence) rate. Their rate of concordance was only 50 per cent.
- Most of the twin studies were done by advertising in gay periodicals. This naturally raises the percentage of instances of homosexuality among the twins, as the likelihood of sample bias drastically increases. As researchers Stanton Jones and Mark Yarhouse observe, "Homosexuals who had homosexual twins may have been more likely to volunteer than those who did not. This is the problem that researchers call sample bias—if the study method tends to recruit gay twins who have gay co-twins more than those who have twin siblings who are not gay, then the findings may be biased."[5]
- It has to be asked how much of a role environment plays, as each set of twins was raised in the same home and environment. In my estimation, SSM advocates undervalue the role a person's upbringing plays in this. I believe that environment plays a primary role in the increasing incidence of homosexuality today.
- If homosexuality is genetic, it would almost certainly die out or decline drastically, as homosexuals procreate at a much lower

incidence. Therefore, it should be found in an increasingly smaller percentage of people as time progresses.

- Michael Bailey subsequently refuted this twin study when he sent surveys to every twin in Australia by using the Australian Twin Registry. This enabled him to eliminate the potential for sample bias. What he discovered was that the concordance rate of homosexuality among identical twins dropped from the 52 per cent of the first study to 20 per cent in this second, more accurate, study. This almost eliminates the possibility that homosexuality is a purely genetic trait. Instead, it strongly points to upbringing and environmental influences as factors that significantly increase the likelihood of homosexual orientation.

In recent years, there has been a lot more noise out of SSM promoters concerning studies of animal sexuality, especially as it relates to homosexuality. From the Bonobo monkey to "gay sheep," such research attempts to link animal behavior to human sexual behavior. But this research is based on rare exceptions to the norm and is anchored in evolutionary presuppositions. In any case, animal behavior is guided by instinct not rational thought. By using the same brand of evolutionary logic, what other human behaviors might find justification?

Since some animals commit infanticide (filicide) or engage in cannibalism, perhaps we shouldn't be too alarmed when we see the same behavior in humans? Some years ago, two US academics wrote a book entitled *A Natural History of Rape: Biological Bases of Sexual Coercion*[6] which essentially rationalized rape on the basis of residual animal instincts and evolutionary hangover. I have yet to hear of anyone using this defense in a rape case.

It is as unreasonable as it is unscientific to attribute human psychodynamics to unusual animal behavior. The zoo is the last place humans should go for advice on moral matters and social policy concerning marriage and family.

That some in the homosexual movement resort to such fallow logic evidences a level of desperation that will go to almost any lengths to legislate and coerce acceptance of homosexuality.

One final study of note is that of Alfred Kinsey in the late 1940s. Many gay activists still quote from Kinsey's fatally flawed research. Kinsey maintained that 10 per cent of the population in America was gay in the 1940s. Yet few who promote this flawed statistic will tell you that, of Kinsey's 5,300 test subjects, some 25 per cent were prison inmates. Others were male prostitutes. In other words, he sampled a section of the population that was hardly representative of the mainstream populace. Kinsey's findings are riddled with gross sample bias and can hardly be taken seriously. Surprisingly, there are still those who quote Kinsey with authority.[7]

So what has science really proved? In the words of scientists themselves:

- "Homosexuality is not purely genetic ... Environmental factors play a role. There is not a single master gene that makes people gay ... I don't think we will ever be able to predict who will be gay."[8]

- "A nationwide University of Chicago study of sexuality in America in 1994 concluded, '... it was patently false that homosexuality is a uniform attribute across individuals, that is stable over time, and that it can be easily measured.' Studies across the globe that have now sampled 100,000 individuals have found the same ... We now know that in the majority of both men and women, 'homosexuality' as defined by any scientifically rigorous criteria, spontaneously tends to 'mutate' into heterosexuality over the course of a lifetime. The proportion of people who adopt a homosexual identity and the length of time they persist in holding on to it are affected primarily by environmental factors ... These factors—deemed 'cultural' or 'demographic'—include effects such as social networks, education, early sexual experiences, childhood sexual abuse, and cultural beliefs."[9]

- "There is no research supporting a genetic basis of homosexuality. The work of [Chandler] Burr has been discredited by *Scientific American*, the brain study of Simon Levay has been discredited. They're desperate to find the biological causes. There are none."[10]

Significantly, none of the scientific studies conducted has proven a biological or genetic causation for homosexuality. The only accomplishment is that now more questions are being asked. Dogmatically to maintain that a person is born gay is as disingenuous as it is misleading.

When robbed of this fallacy, the rest of the arguments offered by the gay community fall like dominos.

It is no surprise, therefore, that gay activists militantly insist on the notion of genetic orientation. Their whole agenda relies upon the perceived reality of an "undeniable" biological link to homosexuality. As Mark Yarhouse concludes, "The more people believed that homosexuality was a biological 'given' the more likely they were to support a variety of issues deemed important to some in the gay community (e.g. ordination of practicing gay, lesbian, or bisexual clergy; gay rights legislation, etc.)."[11]

Presupposition 2: Discrimination. Is it always wrong to judge?
If homosexuality is an inborn trait, then it is nothing short of discrimination, tantamount to racism, to oppose such behavior. Thus, homosexuals invoke slavery/apartheid[12] arguments to castigate and tar their detractors. But this is a non sequitur. The logical sums they use just don't add up, because morality is not bigotry. We could not live without making moral judgments on a regular basis.

The white man or woman is born that way and can never change his or her skin color (unless he or she is rich). The Bible condemns racism because God has made from one man all nations, and all people on earth today are descendants of Adam and Eve through Noah and his wife. Further, he condemns all manner of sexual sin because it perverts his creation mandate for marriage and sexuality.[13]

Judgment based on discernment is not necessarily pejorative or condemnatory in nature. Judgment is really about making distinctions. As Young and Nathanson rightly conclude, "There could be no such thing as a culture without the ability to make distinctions ... The human condition does not permit perfect equality ... If discrimination in the case of marriage is evil, then it is surely the lesser of two evils."[14] Their point is simple: ideological utopia doesn't exist. It is impossible to live life without making moral distinctions.

Those who are honest will admit they make a multitude of discriminations (discernments) on any given day. We simply could not live without making such distinctions. How many parents would knowingly hire a babysitter who was a known pedophile? How many parents would send their kids to a youth club run by a group of neo-Nazis and skinheads? Would you let your daughter date a known drug lord or gang leader? No; in all three cases you would make the necessary distinctions—or what we call moral judgments.

The only people who don't make any judgments are those who have departed this life for the next. As was noted earlier, to oppose sexual immorality is not the equivalent of condemning sexuality. One must discern between God's holy standards for sexuality and the world's blurring of God's distinctives for the same.

Presupposition 3: Transvaluation. What is a transvaluationist?

Though the term "transvaluation" is not commonly used today, it is still a very apt description of the SSM lobby. A transvaluationist is simply a person who reverses commonly held beliefs and definitions. This means that he or she calls what is black, "white," and light, "dark," and good, "evil," and evil, "good." It is the logical conclusion for the relativists' creed. As the book of Isaiah says, "Woe to those who call evil good, and good evil; Who substitute darkness for light and light for darkness; Who substitute bitter for sweet and sweet for bitter" (Isa. 5:20).

This is why much of what the Bible labels "sin," like homosexuality, is now widely accepted and promoted as cardinal virtues. At the same time, those who hold to the biblical perspective are seen as the ones committing the unpardonable sin, because they refuse to transvalue or change God's holy standards.

To arrive at the conclusions they do, transvaluationists have to be subjectively guided by their emotions. How one feels becomes more important than what one thinks. Indeed, in this postmodern world, we are feeling a lot these days, but, as David Wells concludes, "We aren't feeling so well"![15]

Presupposition 4: Deconstructionism. Does the Bible really say that?

Deconstructionists strip history of its facts and significance, empty words of meaning, neuter morality and use backward logic to try to prove their point. There are no absolutes, so you create your own temporary truths.

You impose your own self-styled meaning on everything. You guide history and word meanings toward the desired objective and tweak things as you go.[16]

As Humpty Dumpty said in Lewis Carroll's book *Through the Looking Glass*, "'When I use a word … it means just what I choose it to mean, neither more nor less.' 'The question is,' said Alice, 'whether you *can* make words mean so many different things.' 'The question is,' said Humpty Dumpty, 'which is to be master—that's all.'"[17] Here Lewis Carroll brilliantly illustrates the deconstructionists' hermeneutic. This is precisely how gay theologians interpret the Bible. They eisegetically (i.e. subjectively imposing their feelings on the text) deconstruct biblical context, word meanings, cultural background, grammar, and syntax to suit their sexual objectives. This is all replaced with their sexual bias.

Here are a few brief examples of their skew interpretations:

1. SSM interpreters maintain that the sin of Sodom and Gomorrah in Genesis 19 is of "inhospitality" on the part of Sodom's welcoming committee, rather than homosexuality. The SSM interpreter is heavily reliant on current culture and various philosophical streams of existential thought. This leads to the exchange of word meanings, while critical aspects of a verse's context are ignored. Genesis 19:5 illustrates this well: SSM advocates erroneously claim the phrase "that we may know [*yada*] them" (KJV) refers to hospitality. Yet 19:8 uses *yada* in an obviously sexual context. The SSM lobby conveniently avoids 19:8 when interpreting 19:5. When clipped of its normal context, verse 5 can be interpreted to suit the reader's own context.

In the end, does the penalty God attached to this sin of "inhospitality" seem a bit excessive? After all, God completely destroyed both Sodom and Gomorrah. As F. LaGard Smith humorously notes, the gay community would have us believe that the sin here was simply a case of "… a chamber of commerce welcoming committee gone wrong."[18]

2. More incriminating evidence against homosexuality is found in Leviticus 18:22 and 20:13. These two passages respectively declare,

You shall not lie with a male as one lies with a female; it is an abomination. (Lev. 18:22)

If there is a man who lies with a male as those who lie with a woman, both of them have committed a detestable act; they shall surely be put to death. Their bloodguiltiness is upon them. (Lev. 20:13)

Pro-gay theologians try to nullify these verses by maintaining that these laws were purity laws that regulated Israel's ceremonial worship in the tabernacle and later in the temple. Yet violation of purity laws was never a capital offense as Leviticus 20:13 indicates of homosexuality.[19] In maintaining this view, pro-gay theologians create the impression that the above verses are no different from the dietary laws in Leviticus 11. What it is crucial to understand here is that this would mean there was no real moral significance attached to these laws.

What pro-gay commentators fail to acknowledge is that the whole of Leviticus 18 is devoted to regulating sexuality in the family. God was vitally concerned with perpetuating the Genesis 1 and 2 template for marriage and the nation of Israel as they entered the Promised Land. Why? For as the family goes, so goes Israel as a nation. This required certain sexual proscriptions that would help promote his holiness in the family unit, which would then serve as a preservative in the marriage relationship. This, in turn, would benefit society at large. There were proscriptions related to incest, rape, adultery, and bestiality included in the context. Does this mean these are now nullified as well? As the following passage from Leviticus 18:24–30 clearly details, the Canaanites were expelled from the land because of their immorality, not because they were ceremonially unclean:

Do not defile yourselves by any of these things; for by all these the nations which I am casting out before you have become defiled. For the land has become defiled, therefore I have brought its punishment upon it, so the land has spewed out its inhabitants. But as for you, you are to keep My statutes and My judgments and shall not do any of these abominations, neither the native, nor the alien who sojourns among you (for the men of the land who have been before you have done all these abominations, and the land has become defiled); so that the land will not spew you out, should you defile it, as it has spewed out the nation which has been before you. For whoever does any of these abominations, those persons who do so shall be cut off from among their people. Thus you are to keep My charge, that you do not practice any of the abominable customs which have been practiced before you, so as not to defile yourselves with them; I am the LORD your God.

Undoubtedly, God is intent on preserving the family unit in accordance with the parameters he outlined in Genesis 1 and 2. The Levitical laws promoting the sanctity of marriage and family are entirely moral. For this reason they can hardly be compared with the dietary laws, which we well know the New Testament abolishes (see Col. 2:15–17).

3. Some pro-gay sources now promote the idea that Romans 1:24–28 addresses heterosexuals who engage in homosexual activity, not homosexuals who were born (oriented) that way. So the only real sin committed is when a heterosexual experiments with homosexual practices. The argument here is predicated on the notion that Paul was ignorant of what modern-day science has supposedly proved about homosexuality being biologically determined. This is further proof of pro-gay scholars rejecting the authority of God's Word as revelation.

But in verses 27 and 28 the term "unnatural" or "against nature" (*para phusin*) is used to show God's perspective on homosexuality. It simply means that this type of same-sex activity is contrary to God's created design and purpose for his image-bearing creatures. It goes against the grain of his creation order and mandate. To surmise that the reference here is to the person's own nature as a heterosexual is to fly directly in the face of 2,000 years of interpretation of this passage.

Their argument begs the question of bisexuality. What about bisexuals? Are they now excluded from same-sex contact or do they have a consigned genetic predisposition toward their peculiar proclivities as well? Such argumentation evidences a complete disdain for the authority of God's Word as divine revelation. If the Bible is divine revelation—and Jesus Christ himself asserted that it is—then, ultimately, Paul's judgment on the matter is really God's mind as well.

4. Pro-gay advocates are quick to note that the Gospels never address homosexuality. This amounts to an argument from silence. One could easily counter that there are many things not mentioned in the Gospels that society today does frown upon. Does it mean that, if the Gospels don't

mention something like pedophilia or bestiality, these are now fair game as well? If not, why not?[20]

From this brief sampling of passages we can only conclude that the homosexual hermeneutic is incorrect. As Al Mohler poignantly explains, the conclusions of pro-gay theologians require "... feats of exotic biblical interpretation worthy of the most agile circus contortionist ... Revisionists must deny the obvious and argue the ridiculous."[21] Their interpretative methodology amounts to nothing more than hermeneutical acrobatics.[22]

If pro-gay theologians honestly followed the conventional rules of the historical–grammatical (literal) method of interpretation, they would be forced to conclude that homosexuality always was, is, and always will be a sin in God's eyes—a forgivable sin.

In a 2006 court case that had to determine whether or not a burrito was a sandwich, the judge in the case used the literal method of interpretation to determine his verdict. The judge cited *Webster's Dictionary* to define terms, as well as using expert testimony from chefs and culinary historians. After defining words, looking at the historical precedent, and establishing the context, he ruled that a burrito is not a sandwich. One culinary witness in the case testified that to "... call a burrito a sandwich ... the notion is absurd to any credible chef or culinary historian."[23]

When applying this same literal method of interpretation to the Bible by defining words, examining the historical background, using normal rules of grammar and syntax, and establishing the context of a given passage, it all leads to the unmistakable conclusion that, where homosexuality and SSM are concerned, the church has been right for over 2,000 years. Any other notion is absurd.

Presupposition 5: Political legitimacy. What is the goal of SSM?

What is it that SSM advocates really want? They want political validation and legislated acceptance of homosexuality so that they can do whatever they want, whenever they want, and with whomever they want. This is well illustrated in Scandinavia. After legalizing their version of SSM, very few gays availed themselves of matrimony. Why? Because SSM is not primarily about marriage, but about social and cultural approval for homosexuality.

More to the point, Michelangelo Signorile explained in *Out* magazine,

The trick is, gay leaders and pundits must stop watering the issue down—"this is simply about equality for gay couples"—and offer same-sex marriage for what it is: an opportunity to reconstruct a traditionally homophobic institution by bringing it to our more equitable queer value system … Our gay leaders must acknowledge that gay marriage is just as radical and transformative as the religious Right contends it is.[24]

The ultimate objective is nothing less than coerced acceptance of the gay lifestyle and mores. They want to legislate our attitudes and opinions about homosexuality. To this end, SSM advocates are hyper-political and extremely media savvy. It is time for the church of Jesus Christ to wake up and realize that SSM has never been solely about marriage. The issue of marriage is simply a convenient means to a desired end.[25]

This is all illustrated in my South African context by a recent article that appeared in the *Cape Argus* newspaper. The local gay activists are now lamenting that certain churches and denominations will not perform their same-sex ceremonies. The spokesperson for The Triangle Project concluded by saying, "This is no longer simply a gay rights issue. It is now a human rights issue."[26]

Notes

1 Two academics in the USA, **Craig Palmer** and **Randy Thornhill,** wrote a book promoting the idea that men who rape are probably suffering from evolutionary hangover, so there is some biological impetus. Does that morally justify rape? In contradiction to their thesis, the authors claim it does not. For more information on their book, *A Natural History of Rape: Biological Bases of Sexual Coercion*, see the following interview with Palmer from a Christian perspective: **John Lofton,** "Rape and Evolution: Evolution Shows its True Colours," *Creation Magazine*, 23:4 (2001), pp. 50–53. Also available at creationontheweb.com.

2 Quoted in **David Gelman et al.,** "Born or Bred?" *Newsweek*, February 24, 1992, p. 48.

3 Quoted in **Dr. Bill Maier** and **Glenn T. Stanton,** *Marriage on Trial: The Case against Same-Sex Marriage and Parenting* (Downers Grove, IL: IVP, 2004).

4 **Michael J. Bailey, Michael P. Dunne,** and **Nicolas G. Martin,** "Genetic and Environmental Influences on Sexual Orientation and its Correlates in an Australian Twin Sample," *Journal of Personality and Social Psychology*, 78 (March 2000).

5 **Stanton L. Jones** and **Mark A. Yarhouse,** *Homosexuality: The Use of Scientific Research in the Church's Moral Debate* (Downers Grove, IL: IVP, 2000), p. 74.

6 See endnote 1 above.

7 In the 1940s, the proportion of the US population that was homosexual was probably less than 1%. Today, that figure is probably more in the region of 3%, owing (in part) to all the attention this issue has received.

8 **Dean Hamer,** in **Maier** and **Stanton,** *Marriage on Trial*, p. 135.

9 **Dr. Jeffery Satinover,** in **Marvin Olasky,** "Mental Disorder to Civil-Rights Cause, *World Magazine*, February 19, 2005, p. 30.

10 **Dr. Richard Fitzgibbons,** in **D. James Kennedy** and **Jerry Newcombe,** *What's Wrong with Same-Sex Marriage?* (Wheaton, IL: Crossway, 2004).

11 **Mark A. Yarhouse,** "Homosexuality, Ethics, and Identity Synthesis," *Christian Bioethics*, 10 (2004), p. 241.

12 See question 8 in Appendix 2 for an explanation of the slavery/apartheid arguments pro-gay theologians use to tie homosexuality to those issues.

13 Even after God unequivocally declared the church to be racially diverse and nationally inclusive, he reaffirmed the proscription against illicit sexual activity—including homosexuality.

14 **Katherine K. Young** and **Paul Nathanson,** "Marriage à la Mode: Answering Advocates of Gay Marriage," 2003, p. 11, at marriageinstitute.ca.

15 **David F. Wells,** *Losing our Virtue: Why the Church Must Recover its Moral Vision* (Grand Rapids, MI: Eerdmans, 1998), p. 107.

16 "Deconstruction" was a philosophy heavily promoted by French linguist Jacques Derrida. Essentially, "deconstructionism" is a skeptical approach to hermeneutics (interpretation). Derrida believed that no literary theory or methodology for interpreting a text was sufficient enough ever to uncover the meaning. Thus, there are no absolutes. Truth becomes illusory or elusive. Ultimately, any meaning one arrives at is only tentative at best. As a result, all interpretations are filled with ambiguity and vagueness. Simply said, words don't have any real meaning. What is ironic is that Derrida wrote all this down to preserve his meaning!

17 Quoted in **Donald J. Wold,** *Out of Order: Homosexuality in the Bible and the Ancient Near East* (Grand Rapids, MI: Baker, 1998), p. 17.

18 **F. LaGard Smith,** *Sodom's Second Coming* (Eugene, OR: Harvest House, 1993), p. 123–124.

19 In the Old Testament, there are some sixteen capital offenses requiring the death penalty, of which homosexuality is one. That said, there isn't one instance recorded in Scripture when the death penalty was carried out against those caught in homosexual acts. It must be remembered that these Old Testament standards for sexuality are a reflection of God's holy character, and the penalties highlight the severity of the sin from God's perspective. That God extends grace to the sinner is evident in both Testaments. In the New Testament, we see Jesus Christ as the fulfillment and end of the Mosaic law (Matt. 5:17–18; Rom. 10:4), meaning he fulfilled the righteous demands of the Law while satisfying the just demands or penalty while on the cross. Though God's standard has not changed, the earthly penalty is waived because of the finished work of Jesus Christ on the cross. The church's method of dealing with unrepented sexual sins, like homosexuality, is church discipline (Matt. 18:15–20), not the death penalty. God is gracious, in that grace, forgiveness, and transformation are available through Jesus Christ for all who repent and believe. Because of God's mercy (withholding what we do deserve), none of us is consumed. As the apostle Paul exuberantly reminds the church, "… where sin increased, grace abounded all the more" (Rom. 5:20). But on judgment day, God will not suspend his righteous and holy standard for the impenitent.

20 See Chapter 1 note 21 for further comment on this point.

21 Albert Mohler Jr., "The Compassion of Truth in Biblical Perspective," [n.d.], at albertmohler.com/article_read.php?cid=7.

22 Tammy Bruce, a conservative lesbian journalist, further illustrated this point when she warned, "Definition is, in fact, everything, and changing reality is the order of the day for moral relativists." She proceeded to illustrate her point by showing how some feminists are now calling young teenage girls "adolescent women." This subtle change in terminology implies that, as "adolescent women," they now have all the rights accorded to adult women, including sexual freedom and reproductive rights. The same sleight of hand routine is used when describing pedophilia as a "child–adult relationship," or, even more innocuously, as an "intergenerational relationship." **Tammy Bruce,** *The Death of Right and Wrong* (New York: Three Rivers, 2003), pp. 193–203.

23 "Is a Burrito a Sandwich? Judge Says No," November 10, 2006, at foxnews.com/wires/2006Nov10/0,4670,BurritoorSandwich,00.html.

24 Michelangelo Signorile, "I Do, I Do, I Do, I Do, I Do," *Out*, May 1996, pp. 30–32.

25 Recent statistics from countries that recognize SSM or its equivalent indicate a real decline in SSM once the initial aura wears off. After Sweden legalized same-sex unions there were fewer than 1,526 registered gay partnerships between 1993 and 2001. Similarly, in Norway there were 1,293 same-sex partnerships between 1995 and 2003. Norway has only seven same-sex unions for every thousand heterosexual weddings. In Sweden the ratio is 5 to 1,000. See "Family Research Abstract of the Week: Homosexual Unions: Rare and Fragile," April 17, 2007, at worldcongress.org. In the state of Massachusetts, where SSM was legalized in 2004, there were 6,121 same-sex marriages that year. By 2005 this number drastically declined to 2,060. In 2006 there were only 1,427. From January through April of 2007 there were only eighty-seven. Why the rapid decline? Because SSM is not about marriage, it is about destroying the traditionally Christian idea of the family. See Michael Foust, "Mass. 'Gay Marriage' Numbers Plummet," May 25, 2007, at bpnews.net. Also see Timothy J. Daily, Ph.D., "Comparing the Lifestyle of Homosexual Couples to Married Couples," p. 7, at frc.org. This all indicates that SSM is not primarily about the desire for gays to marry.

26 Here was my response to The Triangle Project's absurd statement: "Marriage is a Privilege, Not a Human Right," *Cape Argus*, May, 21 2007, Letters Section: "As a pastor I found the comments of Vista Kalipa ('Churches Ban Gay Marriage,' 17-05-07) telling. According to Kalipa and Triangle Project, marriage is now a 'human rights issue.' I have always approached marriage as a God-given privilege. As such, there are a host of reasons why I won't marry some couples—being same-sex is but one. If I don't think a couple is ready, or prepared, or fails to meet other biblical criteria, my policy is simple: I am not obligated to marry them. To date none of those I have turned away have ever died, gone hungry, suffered from lack of shelter, or been psychologically harmed as a result of my policy. Since marriage is now a 'human rights' issue, what about the following scenarios: 1. Refusing to marry polygamists, which is technically legal here? 2. A case of pedogamy, whereby an intergenerational couple, ages 12 and 50, wish to marry. They are both consenting, loving, and the 12-year-old has a signed permission slip from his or her parents. Am I obligated to marry them? 3. In the UK, animal rights activists have filed a court case on behalf of a chimp, to accord the chimp 'human rights' status. If chimps are granted 'human rights,' would their human rights be violated if I refused to marry them? In the end, Kalipa's absurd statement has more to do with trying to legislate opposing thought than human rights. For this reason I urge all truly God-fearing pastors and denominations to lovingly, yet firmly, stand true to their God-given convictions, and to obey God rather than man (Acts 5:29)!" (Note: The court case involving the chimp was actually to take place in Vienna. It was a British paper that reported it.)

What are some of the primary dangers posed by legalized SSM?

There are many on the sidelines of the SSM issue who wonder what all the fuss is about. Wanting to avoid confrontation, they wonder why we can't just let bygones be bygones? Live and let live. The logic is that, if we just concede for the sake of peace, the whole thing will blow over. But will it? What is really at stake? The following explanation and examples show that the very fabric of society is now on the edge of a precipice.

Giving marriage an extreme makeover

SSM is about redefining and recreating both marriage and the family. In the process, marriage will be revolutionized right out of existence, or at least eclipsed by the new and improved "alternative family." Marriage will be reduced to nothing more than a mere "lifestyle" choice.

Peter Jones, in his book *Pagans in the Pews*, illustrates the concern about this radical makeover for marriage when he quotes radical feminist and lesbian Virginia Ramey Mollenkott:

... "Patriarchy is a profoundly mistaken social system that has caused misery to millions and could yet cause the destruction of humankind and the planet we share ... Compulsory heterosexuality is the very backbone that holds patriarchy together ... If society is to turn from patriarchy to partnership" we must learn that lesbian, bisexual and gay issues are not just private bedroom matters of "doing whatever turns you on." They are "wedges driven into the superstructure of the heteropatriarchal system."[1]

The SSM lobby is very clear about what its goal is. But most people are ignorant of the ramifications for both society and culture. By the time many wake up, it will already be too late.

The detrimental impact on society

When the basic building block of society is destroyed, what will be the outcome? If Scandinavia is anything to go by, marriage will become almost extinct. It will be on the endangered species list. The majority of children now born in Sweden and Norway are born out of wedlock. In Denmark, 60 per cent of firstborn children are illegitimate. In the more liberal districts of Norway, marriage is almost non-existent. What has produced such an overt rejection of marriage? The discarding of marriage has been fueled by the same egalitarian, anti-authoritarian, transvalued, pansexual attitudes that have granted SSM the credence it has attained.

This, over time, will have far-reaching implications for these countries. They will someday find out that by solving one "inequality" they have created more problems than they have solved. By then it will be impossible to put the toothpaste back into the tube.[2]

Canada has embraced SSM, but the Canadians are now beginning to realize they have opened Pandora's proverbial box. In South Africa, in a *Cape Times* article in 2005, it was noted that there is a new political party in Canada called the Sex Party. Their platform is as follows: "'a sex positive culture,' promising to teach children to have sexual activity 'in a gradual way' and to repeal what it calls sex-negative laws such as banning nudity … The Sex Party would create Eros Day to replace a provincial holiday in honour of Queen Victoria … [At] a recent Sex Party fund-raiser … the audience viewed couples having sex, erotic art and provocative performance artists."[3]

Once the door to amorality is open, you are powerless to stop whoever or whatever walks in after you. The Netherlands, which has had SSM since December 2000, illustrates the point. There is now a political party headed by Dutch pedophiles which is pushing for the legal age of sexual relations to be dropped from sixteen to twelve. They also want to see child pornography legalized along with bestiality.[4]

The sexualizing of the Dutch culture has produced unintended consequences, as illustrated by the news headline "Sex, the currency of Dutch teens."[5] The article laments the sad fact that teenage boys in the Netherlands are using young girls for sexual favors in exchange for clothes, jewelry, and other material goods. What is surprising is not that young

Dutch boys are using their female counterparts as convenient objects for sexual desire, but that Dutch authorities are surprised this is happening.

SSM activists scoff at such conclusions, but their dissent will ultimately boomerang back their way.

Persecution and the curbing of religious freedom

SSM will lead to religious persecution and the curbing of religious freedom as we now know and enjoy it. The battle is between religious liberty and gay rights. As one Canadian gay activist said after SSM was legalized, "Freedom of religion will have to give way to the homosexual agenda."[6] That is why, soon after enshrining SSM, Canada instituted hate-speech laws.[7]

Harvard Law professor Mary Ann Glendon notes the irony of all this:

Gay-marriage proponents use the language of openness, tolerance and diversity, yet one foreseeable effect of their success will be to usher in an era of intolerance and discrimination the likes of which we have rarely seen before. Every person and every religion that disagrees will be labeled as bigoted and openly discriminated against. The ax will fall most heavily on religious persons and groups that don't go along.[8]

Young and Nathanson, from Canada, saw the writing on the wall when they warned,

Religious communities would be the first big losers, because religious freedom would become increasingly hard to defend. Even if exceptions were initially made so that religious communities would not be forced to marry gay couples, these exceptions would eventually be challenged in the courts. The latter would have to choose, after all, between two competing rights: freedom of religion versus equality. Guess which one is most likely to trump the other.[9]

This is why pastors have been jailed and/or fined in places like Canada and Sweden.[10] Simply preaching an expository message on a passage like Romans 1:24–28 will get a man fined or incarcerated. Churches that fail to comply with pro-gay legislation will lose their tax-exempt status and face fines; so much for tolerance and freedom of speech.[11]

A watershed for other matrimonial deviancies seeking equality

The probing question SSM advocates have never satisfactorily answered is the one posed by Erwin Lutzer: "If marriage is no longer an exclusive union between a man and a woman, who is to say it must be limited to two people?"[12] I would add that, if the definition of marriage has now expanded to include same-sex couples, why stop there? Why limit it to people? A couple of years ago I called Cape Talk Radio and posed this question. The panel of pro-gay theologians hesitated before the pro-gay Anglican minister gave the stock evasion, "Well, that is a slippery slope we really don't want to go down." Of course not. The slippery slope is theirs alone. And they use this slope like an Olympic bobsled run. By legalizing SSM, the West is boldly going where few have dared to go before, and it is proud of it.

The logical question is that, if SSM is allowed, why not other deviant variations of marriage? What about:

1. POLYGAMY

I am sure there are various religions and cultures that would not object to this. Though the Bible does have a number of examples in the Old Testament of polygamy, in every case one can trace how this deviancy from the Genesis 1 and 2 paradigm led to compounded problems and frustrations resulting in gross family failures. From Abraham to Jacob, and right on through to the judges and King Solomon, polygamous marriages resulted in familial chaos.

2. POLYAMORY

This is group marriage in which any number of "swingers" decide they want all the state and legal benefits of marriage. There are websites devoted to this already. No doubt its supporters will use most of the arguments already marshaled by the gay community to promote legislation of this anything-goes approach to marriage. It is already receiving attention from liberal-minded theologians such as Marvin Ellison, an ordained minister with the Presbyterian Church USA. Ellison asks,

Should marriage, as the legal sanctioning of an intimate sexual affiliation, be limited to two and only two persons, or should room be made for multiple partners who wish to have their intimate relationship recognized and protected by the state? Should religious communities bless multiple coexisting sexual partnerships? Surely one concern with polyamorous affiliations is exploitation, or what feminist critics of polygamy have called an "excess of patriarchy." But how exactly does the number of partners affect the moral quality of a relationship? This question requires a serious answer. Could it be that limiting intimate partnerships to only two people at a time is no guarantee of avoiding exploitation, and expanding them to include more than two parties is no guarantee that the relationship will be exploitative?[13]

This quote evidences that there are already transvalued clerics who are anxious to push the boundaries of marriage beyond the limits of SSM. Such is only a logical conclusion of the philosophy behind SSM. That is why the battle currently being waged in the Anglican Church to ordain gay clergy is so significant. Once this allowance is given, the boundaries will be gradually pushed further to allow for others who are "excluded"—such as transsexuals and polyamorists.

3. ENDOGAMY
This is the union of blood relatives. For genetic and medical reasons, marriage to close blood relatives has been legislated against. If SSM is now allowable, who is to say endogamy is wrong as long as both parties meet the relativistic criteria of mutual love and consent?

4. PEDOGAMY
This is child marriage—or "intergenerational intimacy," as it is euphemistically called. After all, children have rights too. If it is "consensual" and the partners "love" each other, then whose business is it if a twelve-year-old girl weds a fifty-year-old man? Or if an eleven-year-old decides to wed a thirteen-year-old?

"Preposterous," you say. Well, consider the following reminder from one gay advocate, from which much of the gay community tries to distance itself so it doesn't publicly hurt the cause:

The issue of love between men and boys has intersected the gay movement since the late 19th century, with the rise of the first gay-rights movement in Germany. In the United States, as the gay movement has retreated from its vision of sexual liberation, in favor of the integration and assimilation into existing social and political structures, it has increasingly sought to marginalize, even demonize cross-generational love. Pederasty—that is, love between a man and a youth of 12–18 years of age—say middle-class homosexuals, lesbians, and feminists, has nothing to do with gay liberation. Some go so far as to claim, absurdly, that it is a heterosexual phenomenon, or even "sexual abuse." What a travesty! Pederasty is the main form that male homosexuality has acquired throughout Western civilization.[14]

Journalist Andrée Seu offers this commentary on the above quote:

NAMBLA (North American Man/Boy Love Association) may take consolation from such indicators as the tireless work of the Dutch magazine *Paidika* in "normalizing" pedophilia, and in the fact that many countries, connecting the dots between homosexual rights and children's rights, have lowered the age of consent for sex: Britain: age 16, Germany and Italy: age 15; Canada: age 14; Spain, Holland, and Portugal: age 12.[15]

As if this weren't enough, the International Gay and Lesbian Human Rights Commission has already approached the UN to seek a change in the age-of-consent laws—laws against pedophiles.[16] Pedophiles are the next to come out of the closet and to insist on their rights and seek equality on the basis of their consensual love for youngsters.[17]

I am well aware that there are many gay people who stridently disagree with the activists who are pushing things to these extremes. But the logic in this is really quite clear: once you remove the biblical barrier of traditional marriage and the nuclear family, you are powerless to stop the moral landslide that ensues. If there are no absolutes, no fixed reference points, morality becomes an impossibility. It appears that the consequences of the transvaluationist's creed are coming home to roost.

There are many other bizarre examples that illustrate the gross confusion that results when SSM is legitimized and moral absolutes are jettisoned. The following illustrations are representative of the twilight-zone effects of SSM and civil unions:

- In France, a thirty-five-year-old woman became a widow and a bride on the same day when she married her dead boyfriend and then inherited his estate.[18]
- In the Netherlands, a single woman married herself. This raises many questions. What if she wants to divorce herself? One wonders what the honeymoon must have been like.[19]
- In France, it has been reported that some priests have joined in civil solidarity pacts with their housekeepers for the purpose of state benefits.[20]
- The 2004 Pulitzer Prize-winning drama was written about an East German transvestite and entitled *I Am My Own Wife*. Not only do we tolerate such nonsense-on-stilts, but we reward it as well.[21]

It is certain that the relativists' creed is bearing a bountiful harvest. Such eventualities aren't so far-fetched when we consider that in the USA and Europe there are many amoral scholars, such as Peter Singer[22] and Judith Levine, who are aggressively promoting an anything-goes approach toward morality (amorality)—to include pedophilia, bestiality, necrophilia, and polyamory. Their justification is, "As long as it is consensual and it doesn't hurt anyone, it is OK."

Organizations like the Academic Pedophile Advocates (150,000 strong) and NAMBLA are actively lobbying their cause by connecting the dots between homosexual rights and children's rights. On whose coattails do you think these advocacy groups are riding? Whose relativistic logic are they following? Whose anthem are they parroting? The gay community's, of course. After all, most of these champions of amorality first fought for gay rights and SSM.[23]

The associated health risks of the gay lifestyle

Homosexuality is far from a healthy lifestyle, but this isn't commonly reported as the gay community would be stigmatized as a result. So the media, the academic elite, and most medical professionals and politicians have all taken a vow of silence on this subject. It has become taboo. The moment you mention this dirty little secret, the personal attacks begin.

Shouts of "homophobe" and "fundamentalist" become the order of the day. Yet the statistics in the West bear testimony to the fact that the gay lifestyle carries significant health risks.[24] Much of the HIV/AIDS in the West is attributable to the gay lifestyle.

In Africa the situation is different, as HIV is often spread heterosexually. Yet, in the white community of South Africa, most cases of HIV/AIDS are still directly related to homosexuality and intravenous drug usage.

Notes

1 **Peter Jones,** *Pagans in the Pews* (Ventura, CA, Regal, 2001), p. 161.

2 Author **Daniel Heimbach,** in his book *True Sexual Morality: Recovering Biblical Standards for a Culture in Crisis*, goes into some detail about a study conducted by J. D. Unwin early in the twentieth century. Unwin studied eighty-six civilizations, both large and small, over a 5,000-year period. He noted that societies began with high standards for sexual conduct with a limit of one partner in marriage for life. This provided the strength and stability for society. As subsequent generations rose to power, this standard was gradually eroded and the various societies correspondingly weakened and declined. Unwin notes that, "In the beginning, each society had the same ideas in regard to sexual regulations. Then the same strengths took place; the same sentiments expressed; the same results ensued. Each society reduced its sexual opportunity to a minimum and, displaying great social energy, flourished greatly. Then it extended its sexual opportunity [lowered standards]; its energy decreased, and faded away. The one outstanding feature of the whole story is its unrelieved monotony." *True Sexual Morality: Recovering Biblical Standards for a Culture in Crisis* (Wheaton, IL: Crossway, 2004), p. 347.

3 "No Sex Please, We're Canadians: Sex Party Hard Put to Get Rise out of Voters," *The Cape Times*, May 18, 2005, p. 4.

4 Dutch pedophiles have organized themselves into a political party called The Charity, Freedom, and Diversity Party (NVD). As part of their party platform they want to drop the age for sexual consent to twelve. Their rationale is that "A ban just makes children curious." They also go on to advocate everything from child pornography to bestiality. "Dutch Paedophiles to Launch Political Party," May 30, 2006, at iol.co.za.

5 SAPA, "Sex, the Currency of Wayward Dutch Teens", November 11, 2008, at iol.co.za.

6 Cited in **Erwin W. Lutzer,** *The Truth about Same-Sex Marriage: 6 Things You Need to Know about What's Really at Stake* (Chicago: Moody Press, 2004), p. 10.

7 Those in the gay community are often quick to point out that they are the victims of hate crimes. This is sadly true. But what most do not know is that, according to the FBI, among those crimes classified as hate crimes in the USA in 2005, 14% were because of sexual orientation, while 16% were committed because of religion. See **Charles Montaldo,** "FBI Reports 7,163 Hate Crimes in 2005," October 19, 2006, at about.com.

8 Cited in **D. James Kennedy** and **Jerry Newcombe,** *What's Wrong with Same-Sex Marriage?* (Wheaton, IL: Crossway, 2004), p. 69.

9 **Katherine K. Young** and **Paul Nathanson,** "Marriage à la Mode: Answering Advocates of Gay Marriage," 2003, p. 13, at marriageinstitute.ca.

10 See the following sobering article that details some of those who have been dragged into court or fired for their biblical convictions on the issue of homosexuality. Simply sharing the gospel has gotten some fired: "What will be Illegal when Homosexuality is Legal?" November 27, 2008, at wayoflife.org.

11 In an interview in 2006, Elton John blamed "religion" for the hatred and angst leveled at the gay movement ("Ban Organised Religion," November 12, 2006, at news.bbc.co.uk). During the interview, Jake Shears of Scissor Sisters made the interesting comment to Elton John that it was time for gays to quit worrying about the gay-rights movement and to start focusing on the "fundamentalist movements." Presumably his notion of a fundamentalist is anyone who believes that the Bible is God's Word and holds to a literal interpretation of it. See **Jake Shears,** "When Elton Met Jake," November 12, 2006, at observer.guardian.co.uk.

12 **Lutzer,** *The Truth about Same-Sex Marriage*, p. 29.

13 **Marvin M. Ellison,** *Same-Sex Marriage? A Christian Analysis* (Cleveland, OH: Pilgrim, 2004), p. 155.

14 Quoted by **Andrée Seu** "Connecting the Dots," December 27, 2003, at worldmag.com.

15 Ibid. The actual ages of sexual consent for the above-mentioned countries are as follows: Britain: 16; Germany: 14; Italy: 13 if the participants are less than three years apart in age; Canada: 14; Spain: 13; Netherlands: 16; and Portugal: 14 ("Ages of Consent in Europe," en.wikipedia.org; accessed 29 August 2007).

16 **Gene Edward Veith,** "Wandering Shepherds," August 23, 2003, at worldmag.com.

17 Another sordid example of this is given by liberal think-tank elitist Judith Levine, who maintains that "Sex is not harmful to children. It is a vehicle to self-knowledge, love, healing, creativity, adventure, and intense feelings of aliveness. There are many ways even the smallest children can partake of it" (quoted in **Tammy Bruce,** *The Death of Right and Wrong* (New York: Three Rivers, 2003, p. 193). Apparently, South African President Thabo Mbeki agreed, at least in part, with this brand of thinking, as on June 8, 2006 he signed the

Child Act into effect, allowing twelve-year-olds to purchase birth control, receive treatment for STDs, and pursue abortions, all without parental consent. This implies that the age of sexual consent in South Africa is now twelve.

18 **Peter Sprigg,** *Outrage: How Gay Activists and Liberal Judges are Trashing Democracy to Redefine Marriage* (Washington: Regency, 2004), p. 103.

19 This I saw on CNN in July 2003. I would not have believed it had I not seen it reported with my own eyes.

20 **Lutzer,** *The Truth about Same-Sex Marriage*, p. 27. France, like many other European countries, has civil solidarity pacts (or civil unions), which stop short of being fully recognized as marriage but still offer those in such unions all the legal and fiscal privileges of a married couple. This is a government's way of trying to appease both sides of the debate on SSM. This is ultimately why traditional marriage is becoming obsolete in some countries; couples can enter into a civil union for the sake of convenience without the connotations of traditional marriage.

21 **Sprigg,** *Outrage*, p. 103.

22 Peter Singer is an Australian professor of ethics who teaches at Princeton University in New Jersey. He is a consummate relativist who advocates almost any behavior as long it is "loving and consensual."

23 In case you still don't believe that the SSM lobby is out to destroy and redefine marriage, consider the following statement by liberal journalist Michael Kinsley: "The solution is to end the institution of marriage, or rather, the solution is to end the monopoly of marriage. And yes, if three people want to get married, or one person wants to marry herself and someone else wants to conduct a ceremony and declare them married, let 'em. If you and your government aren't implicated, what do you care? If marriage were an entirely private affair, all the disputes over gay marriages would become irrelevant" (**Michael Kinsley,** "Abolish Marriage: Let's Really Get the Government out of our Bedrooms," *Washington Post*, July 3, 2003, A23). What Kinsley won't acknowledge is that our private sins often have very public consequences. When the foundation of society is destroyed, all the rest of us pay the price in a thousand different ways.

24 It is not the purpose of this book to address this issue. For an in-depth treatment on the health risks among gays, see the excellent article by **Dr. John Diggs Jr., MD,** "The Health Risks of Gay Sex," 2002, online as a White Paper at corporateresourcecouncil.org.

4. How did we get here? The cultural creeds that led us to our current situation

We have arrived at our current cultural and societal situation imperceptibly and incrementally over the course of the past forty years. The following five creeds have inexorably and insidiously damaged marriage and family in incalculable ways.

The creed of "free" love has spawned a laissez-faire attitude toward sex and morals. What we are now learning is that, statistically speaking, free love hasn't been very free. It has come with a high price tag attached: cases of rape, child abuse, teenage pregnancy, and sexual abuse of women are all sky high and directly related to the promotion of free love. This doesn't even factor in the emotional trauma and consequences of such reckless behavior. As a pastor, I only get to deal with these matters long after the damage is done. My experience in counseling those caught in this web of deceit is that the term "free love" is another in a long line of transvalued notions that much of society has bought without realizing the cost.[1]

The creed of convenient divorce follows close on the heels of the dogma of free love. This has produced the era of disposable relationships. It gives marriage the air of drive-through convenience. Many rationalizations are used by those who seek an easy way out of a bad relationship. This mindset has cheapened the whole idea of marriage and spawned a great deal of skepticism about marriage in the populace at large.[2]

The creed of feminism is another icon of our current culture that has greatly contributed to promotion of SSM. It was Gloria Steinem, an early pioneer for the feminist cause, who said, "A woman needs a man like a fish needs a bicycle."[3] Ironically, she herself got married. Betty Friedan (National Organization for Women) likened being a housewife to being in a "comfortable concentration camp."[4] Such statements evidence a high degree of cynicism for the God-ordained institution of marriage.[5]

Forty years of radical feminist thought has demeaned masculinity and confused femininity. Now we live in a world where the men have been feminized and the women have been masculinized and many are perplexed about their gender identity. It is in this vacuum that we have seen the rise and promotion of androgyny, transgenderism, transsexuality, and transvestism. These deface the God-given distinctions between the genders. To erase the distinction between male and female is to trivialize God and his image-bearing qualities which are resident in both men and women.

The creed of tolerance is another "value" that is highly esteemed by promoters of SSM. To this I might add "uncritical tolerance." Young and Nathanson give this warning: "... no society could endure if tolerance were taken to its ultimate conclusion: the belief that 'anything goes.' In addition to tolerance—otherwise known as 'love,' 'caring,' or 'compassion'—every society must be guided by wisdom. And that requires citizens to be as reasonable as they are tolerant."[6]

What is meant by the term "tolerance" today is that we accept almost any behavior or thought, no matter how bizarre or off-the-wall—like a woman marrying herself. No judging will be tolerated. Such is the non-sequitur (it doesn't follow), hypocritical logic of our postmodern world.[7]

In large measure, the church's acceptance of homosexuality has been promoted by an aberrant understanding of God's love. The question is often lodged, "Isn't God a loving God?" The logical implication is that, because God is loving, he therefore will not judge the homosexual, or anyone else for that matter. But as John MacArthur so insightfully reminds us, "Love has been redefined as a broad tolerance that overlooks sin and embraces good and evil alike. But this is not love; it is apathy mixed with compromise ... Remember the supreme manifestation of God's love is the cross, where Christ 'loved us and gave himself up for us, a fragrant offering and sacrifice to God.'"[8]

The Bible, not culture, must determine the Christian doctrine of love. God's love is ultimately defined by his other attributes, such as justice, righteousness, mercy, and the like. To divorce God's love from his other defining characteristics is to entertain a warped view of both God and his love. The predominant cultural understanding of God's love more closely resembles the sentimental sonnets one hears from modern pop songs. The pop-song mentality of love is part of the problem, not the solution. Let the cross, not culture, define your view of God's love!

Sadly, the church at large is not always a part of the needed solution to the above-mentioned influences. *The creed of indifference* is partly to blame for the atmosphere that endorses SSM. In short, the church has let its guard down while timidly failing to speak the truth in love: "Homosexuality has risen to the top of the social policy agenda because of the utter wreck we all have made of family life over the past fifty years."[9]

The one institution that should have been leading the moral vanguard in the opposite direction to SSM is the church. But the church has been too busy celebrating its new-found "freedoms." As 1 Peter 4:17 declares, "For it is time for judgment to begin with the household of God; and if it begins with us first, what will be the outcome for those who do not obey the gospel of God?"

A defective view of the Bible (bibliology) and an incorrect, philosophically laden hermeneutic (method of interpretation) have contributed, in large part, to the dilemma we now face. The result is that many mainline denominations are split over this issue. Most recently, the Dutch Reformed Church in South Africa endorsed "non-practicing homosexuals" in the ministry.[10] This issue of SSM does not provide the luxury of taking a middle ground. To sit on the fence here, as many in the church are doing, is tacitly to endorse the SSM creed. Once the first concession to homosexuality and SSM is made, the journey down the slippery slope has begun, with little hope of return.[11] Now that the camel has forced its head into the tent, we must all prepare for a very restless night.

Notes

1 See Appendix 3, "Heads up from the Headlines," which cites many present-day examples of the fruits of free love.

2 Some SSM advocates go to great lengths to try to convince their readers and themselves that SSM will somehow strengthen the whole institution of marriage. From a biblical perspective, SSM cheapens and trivializes the "one man and one woman for a lifetime" concept. I believe

that, in time, statistics will reveal a very unflattering view of SSM in this regard.

3 Cited by **Robert Heskett,** "Gloria Steinem Got Married!", at familynonviolence.org/articles/gloria.html.

4 Cited by **Wendy McElroy,** "Saying 'No' to Feminist Stereotypes," July 11, 2001, at foxnews.com/story/0,2933,29161,00.html.

5 This is not to say that bad marriages aren't prevalent today. In South Africa, the headlines bear testimony to the fact that domestic abuse and violence are on the rise. This is, in part, because many couples get married for all the wrong reasons. Add to this substance abuse and ignorance about biblical principles for governing the marriage relationship, and you have the recipe for relationship ruin. Feminism has further added to the crisis in failing marriages by promoting gender confusion.

6 **Katherine K. Young** and **Paul Nathanson,** "Marriage à la Mode: Answering Advocates of Gay Marriage," 2003, p. 16, at marriageinstitute.ca.

7 What I disagree with is not tolerance itself, but the *uncritical* or *mindless* tolerance that has become so pervasive and produced many decisions and actions that can only be described as nonsense-on-stilts. Certainly, I agree with social tolerance, meaning that I respect one with whom I may stridently disagree. In addition, I can support the notion of legal tolerance, which is the right for a person to follow whatever faith he or she wants. What I reject here is the uncritical tolerance that has produced the relativists' creed that, ironically, targets those who vigorously disagree with them.

8 **John MacArthur,** "God's Word on Homosexuality: The Truth about Sin and the Reality of Forgiveness," *The Master's Seminary Journal*, 19:2 (2008), p. 155.

9 **Dr. Jeffery Satinover,** in **Marvin Olasky,** "Mental Disorder to Civil-Rights Cause, *World Magazine*, February 19, 2005, *World Magazine*, p. 31.

10 The term "non-practicing homosexual" is an oxymoron. Given the unbridled desire that usually accompanies the lifestyle, it is unrealistic and naïve for the Dutch Reformed Church (DRC) to think that such is possible. This is well illustrated by a recent event in the Evangelical Lutheran Church in America (ELCA). ELCA had a similar position to that of the DRC. But it (ELCA) has now urged bishops to refrain from defrocking gay and lesbian ministers who violate the celibacy rule. This has allowed defrocked ministers, such as Bradley Schmeling at St. John's Lutheran Church in Atlanta, to go back to work. Schmeling called this decision a "crack in the dam." No doubt the DRC will follow suit in the days to come. My question for the DRC hierarchy is: How is it going to police this? Taking such a position is only trying to appease both sides of the debate. Compromises are fine where preferences are involved. But when moral principle is at stake, compromise poisons the well. Such is the case here. See

Dorie Turner, "Lutheran Congregation Keeps Gay Pastor," August 12, 2007, at washingtonpost.com/wp-dyn/content/article/2007/08/12/AR2007081201041.html.

11 My humble advice for those in denominations and churches that have conceded very valuable ground in this debate is to flee, just as Lot fled Sodom. Then find a church that unapologetically preaches the whole counsel of God's Word. Second Corinthians 6:14–7:1 makes it clear that fellowship is not possible when the constraining love of Christ (2 Cor. 5:14) has been obscured by worldly thinking and ungodly cultural accommodation. Once a church or denomination makes such cultural accommodations, we know that the authority of God's Word has long since been abandoned and that a relativistic hermeneutic has been adopted. This is the only way the promotion of homosexuality and SSM can be endorsed. Quite frankly, once the doors to SSM are flung open, the battle to reverse it has probably already been lost.

5. How should the church respond to SSM? A scriptural strategy for the church

As one might expect, there are many opinions on how the church of Jesus Christ should respond to this current crisis. Though a whole book could be written on this topic alone, what follows are just a few of the key starting points that the Bride of Christ needs to consider as she faces the issue of SSM.[1]

Shepherds must begin feeding their flocks on all the vital issues and true doctrines concerning marriage and family. This presupposes a belief in the authority of God's Word and a historical–grammatical (literal) interpretation as a vital starting point. Once this is established, pastors need to teach their people what the Bible says about marriage and family. If God ordained marriage, we need to let God, not psychology or politics, define what it is and what it is not. This means vigorous pre-marital counseling, marriage-counseling classes for those already married, and helping marriages that we know are in trouble.

One of the primary reasons why so many marriages are in trouble today is because pastors will marry anyone who asks. It has become a money-making industry for some, while others are fearful of the consequences of saying "no" to couples who may not be ready. We need to have biblically derived standards for marrying couples. There have been several couples I have refused to marry because I didn't think they met the biblical criteria, they weren't ready, or they hadn't been through an extensive, biblically based pre-marital counseling course.

In addition, I have learned that, just because people declare that they are born again, it doesn't necessarily mean that they know how to be good husbands or wives. They must "lay aside the old self" and "put on the new self" (Eph. 4:22–24). The church needs proactively to teach its people the biblical principles for marriage and how rightly to relate to one another in the shadow of the cross. This ounce of prevention is worth the proverbial pound of cure.

Further, we need to train our young people and singles about the biblical basis for choosing a mate. They must know that there is something worse than never marrying. It is called a bad marriage. The Bible, not one's emotional incontinence, must be the guide if a world of woe is to be avoided. But this won't happen unless pastors and church leaders teach what the Bible has to say on this most important issue of marriage. Then pastors need to model godly, Christ-centered marriages. If we exclude this, there is no real hope of turning the corner on failing marriages.

Shepherds must take sexual sin of any nature seriously (Eph. 5:5; Gal. 5:19–21; 1 Cor. 5:5; 6:9–20). We can't afford to wink and look the other way. Sexual sin must be confronted, both in the pew and in the pulpit! Failure here can only be construed as approval of such sin.

It is for this reason that the Marriage Alliance[2] in South Africa lacked moral authority and clout when addressing the SSM initiative. There were churches and denominations that were loudly voicing their opposition to SSM and homosexuality while simultaneously winking at adultery, fornication, cohabitation, and even pedophilia in both the pew and the pulpit. Is it any wonder this movement failed in its quest to convince the South African government about the dangers of SSM? Though I applaud their efforts and support their cause, those in the Marriage Alliance needed to sweep their own porch first.[3] The church needs to repent of all the immoralities that plague her before targeting the gay community. It is high time the church of Jesus Christ rediscovered Matthew 18:15–20 and started applying it to both the pulpit and the pew. This may not be popular, but it is necessary if the church is to strive for purity. It must be remembered that God does not ever use a dirty vessel to begin revival. But, as the gospel declares, there is life-changing forgiveness for all who turn from their sin! The problem today is that most people want to know what it is they need forgiveness for, as sin has been completely deconstructed into a mere lifestyle choice. In this, the church can be most instructive.

Shepherds must take divorce and remarriage more seriously. This goes without saying. Pastors need to encourage couples to settle their differences in a truly biblical way. Experience has taught me that couples having problems have usually swept years' worth of differences and acrimony under the carpet. Now they trip over the carpet every time they enter the house. Many are inclined to take the path of least resistance and just get a divorce.

I once dealt with a woman who was in the midst of a divorce from her husband of more than thirty years. She had been told by her pastor that the exception clause in Matthew 19:9, "except for the cause of adultery," applied to almost any situation. In this particular instance, the husband worked long hours, so the pastor spiritualized work as this man's mistress. Based on gross spiritualizing of Matthew 19:9, this woman was seeking an unbiblical divorce, and was encouraged to do so by a pastor who was so broad in his interpretation of Matthew 19:9 that an aircraft carrier could sail through it.

Rather than walking away from their marriages, couples need to be challenged to honor Christ by seeking reconciliation with each other. After all, if we have been reconciled to Christ Jesus (2 Cor. 5:18–21), who are we to say we won't be reconciled to our husbands or wives? Such thinking is antithetical to the spirit of the gospel. If we have been forgiven for our own mountain of sin by Christ, who are we to begrudge forgiveness to our spouses?[4]

Shepherds must teach what the Bible says about gender distinctions and gender roles. We have a group of men in our local church who meet together. The group is called "Men of Hope," based on 1 Corinthians 16:13, where Paul tells the Corinthian men to "act like men." Men are confused on this point today. We are surrounded by men trying to look and act like women and women trying to look and act like men. There are even men trying to get in touch with their feminine side, whatever that is.[5] Is it any wonder many men are confused? They don't know what it means to be a godly man. We must teach them, but we cannot teach them what we do not know ourselves. Women, likewise, need to be reminded of what it means to be a godly woman. The whole unisex culture has blurred these vital distinctions between the sexes with deleterious effects.

Gay-rights activists are busy sowing further confusion on this front by promoting the use of gender-neutral pronouns and rendering titles like "Mom" and "Dad" obsolete, as same-sex parents find these terms "offensive" and discriminatory. There is also a campaign to create gender-free restrooms, to make the transgendered and transsexual among us feel better about themselves. I guess that former designations like "His" and "Hers" are too demeaning.

Shepherds must equip their people adequately to prepare their children for the sexually saturated world. Our children face a veritable sexual challenge today. If we do not instruct them, the world certainly will. The next generation will need a great deal of biblical input in order to navigate the sexual slalom of life. Pastors can make appropriate materials available to parents to help guide them in instructing their children.[6] Of course, one of the best tools of instruction is for parents to have a healthy marriage and maintain a positive role model for their kids.

Finally, the church must speak up and reach out while speaking the truth in love. We cannot afford to maintain a vow of silence for the sake of some artificial "peace" and "unity."[7] After all, there can be no lasting peace or unity where the truth is not heralded. This issue is not going to go away just because we wish it would. The Bible-believing church needs the courage of her convictions here. The issue of SSM needs to be addressed firmly, convincingly, and lovingly. Biblical counter-measures need to be put into place.

Without this, the church will be consumed by SSM and its detrimental spin-offs. As Alex Montoya from The Master's Seminary in California challenges us,

Finally, the church must be careful not to adopt the customs of the world. What it tolerates today, its children will practice tomorrow. In an age of accommodation and compromise, when churches are more interested in numbers than genuine conversions, the church is in danger of ceasing to make holiness and truth the motivation for its existence. The words of the apostle Paul are a fitting conclusion to this debate on homosexuality: "Let no one deceive you with empty words, for because of these things the wrath of God comes upon the sons of disobedience. Therefore do not be partakers with them; for you were formerly darkness, but now you are children of the light in the Lord; walk as children of light ... Do not participate in the unfruitful deeds of darkness, but instead even expose them; for it is disgraceful even to speak of things which are done by them in secret" (Eph. 5:6–8, 11–12).[8]

The church has embraced the Jesus movement, the Holy Spirit movement, the Toronto Blessing, gold teeth, church growth, the prayer of Jabez, forty days of purpose, and now the emerging church—but can we honestly say we are any better off morally and spiritually because of these movements? The church has become too concerned with the books of man and the opinions of man. It is time to return to the book of God and honestly survey his opinion on this watershed issue. Scripturally saturated minds are powerful agents for change when combined with transformed hearts!

Notes

1 Alex Montoya offers the following battle plan for the church: 1. The church must condemn the sin of homosexuality; 2. The church must convert the homosexual; 3. The church must confront error; and 4. The church must cleanse itself. **Alex D. Montoya,** "Homosexuality and the Church," *The Master's Seminary Journal*, 11:2 (2000), pp. 164–168.

2 The Marriage Alliance is a broad-based Christian coalition that sought to halt the advances of SSM in South Africa. They ultimately failed, as both South Africa's constitution and the Bill of Rights are worded in such a way that it would have been nearly impossible to halt the institution of SSM as the law of the land. For this reason, the Marriage Alliance sought the sanction of civil unions rather than SSM.

3 The following is a letter I wrote in response to the Marriage Alliance. "Church Guilty of Double Standard," *Cape Argus*, June 13, 2006, Letters Section: "Dear Editor, Though I wholeheartedly agree with Errol Naidoo ('Allowing Gay Marriage will Undermine the Foundation of our Society,' June 7, 2006), as a pastor I must demur on one front. Sadly, I know there are many churches that inconsistently and selectively maintain the biblical standards of sexuality and marriage. On the one hand, there are churches that will fight tenaciously against same-sex marriage and homosexuality. Yet, on the other hand, they are hypocritically undermining the same God-ordained institution (marriage) they piously profess to preserve. It is nothing short of crass hypocrisy for churches and pastors to hurl polemics against homosexuality and same-sex marriage while entertaining fornication, cohabitation, adultery, and easy divorce in the pew. What is even worse is when a church turns a blind eye to its pastor in the pulpit, who is guilty of the same (one can be forgiven of such vice, but the consequences of such failures render one disqualified from the ministry). Ironically, by maintaining this double standard, the church at large is contributing to the demise of the

very institution it seeks to save. Until God's people, both in the pew and in the pulpit, consistently apply all that God has to say on matters of sexuality and the sanctity of marriage, how can we expect His blessing in this realm? After all, 'Judgment begins at the house of God'!"

4   This is not to deny that there are sometimes extenuating circumstances, such as abuse, abandonment, and unrepented adultery, that will see a marriage end in divorce. My point here is not to berate those who are divorced, for they need ministering to, but rather to encourage the church at large to do all it can to begin reversing this sad trend.

5   Wiccans and pagans believe that within every person is a combination of male and female—an androgynous mix. If this is true, then each person is complete within him- or herself. This means that men don't need women, and women don't need men. And, contrary to the Genesis 1 and 2 template, Adam was complete without Eve; he just needed to get in touch with his feminine side.

6   See this excellent article that outlines eleven goals for parenting in today's sexual obstacle course: **Richard L. Holland,** "Christian Parenting And Homosexuality," *The Master's Seminary Journal*, 19:2 (2008), pp. 217–231.

7   As Peter Jones admonished concerning the gains of gay rights, "By the power of Christ and His Spirit, preach and witness to this Gospel publicly for all you are worth, both as churches and as individual believers. We cannot allow our mouths to be closed. As Paul said: 'Pray for me that I might open my mouth with boldness … to speak what I must speak' (Eph. 6:20)"; in "Are We Goin' to San Francisco?", August 7, 2007, at truthxchange.com.

8   **Montoya,** "Homosexuality and the Church," p. 168.

6. Is change really possible?

Can homosexuals change? The answer to this question is, of course, yes! Because of God's limitless grace, those in bondage to any sin, including any sexual sin, for that matter, can find forgiveness of sin and the basis for transformation in the finished work of Jesus Christ. Once in Christ, old things are passed away and a person is now a new creature in Christ (2 Cor. 5:17).

1 Corinthians 6:9–11 answers this best:

Or do you not know that the unrighteous will not inherit the kingdom of God? Do not be deceived; neither fornicators, nor idolaters, nor adulterers, nor effeminate, nor homosexuals, nor thieves, nor the covetous, nor drunkards, nor revilers, nor swindlers, will inherit the kingdom of God. Such *were* some of you; but you *were* washed, but you *were* sanctified, but you *were* justified in the name of the Lord Jesus Christ and in the Spirit of our God [emphasis added].

The ancient Greek city of Corinth was world-renowned for its immoralities and sexual vice, but for those who repented and believed on the Lord Jesus Christ there was spiritual as well as physical emancipation from their former ways of life! As the above passage indicates, a gospel that doesn't produce transformative change is no gospel at all.

On this vital point, John MacArthur encourages us to lovingly and faithfully pursue homosexuals with the liberating message of the gospel:

What should be your response to the homosexual? Make it a gospel response—confront him with the truth of Scripture that condemns him as a sinner, and point him to the hope of salvation through repentance and faith in Jesus Christ. Stay faithful to the Lord as you respond to homosexuality by honoring His word, and leave the results to Him.[1]

Homosexuality is not a greater sin than other sins and does not require a different plan on God's part to save and redeem. What the passage from 1 Corinthians teaches us is that there is more grace in God than there is sin in your past! As someone once said, "He is a better Savior than you are a sinner"! The message of amazing grace is exactly what the church needs to promote and practice.

For the homosexual—or anyone else—who needs Christ, the message is clear: come just as you are. When you come just as you are, God's Word promises that you will not leave the same as you came! For God will grant you the ability to become what you never could become on your own—a child of God! "But as many as received Him, to them He gave the right to become children of God, *even* to those who believe in His name, who were born, not of blood nor of the will of the flesh nor of the will of man, but of God" (John 1:12–13).[2]

Notes

1 **John MacArthur,** "God's Word on Homosexuality: The Truth about Sin and the Reality of Forgiveness," *The Master's Seminary Journal*, 19:2 (2008), p. 174.

2 I highly recommend the website harvestusa.org for all those who are gay and want spiritual help, or if you have a family member or close friend who is gay and you need advice on how to respond.

Appendix 1. Legislating homosexuality in school

While working on this book, the following situation in the state of California came to my attention. The so-called anti-discrimination bill that Governor Schwarzenegger just signed into law reinforces some of the key points made in this book: namely, that the gay-rights agenda is not primarily concerned about anti-discrimination laws but in legislating how others think. It is about normalizing attitudes through aggressive indoctrination and social engineering. In the end, there are those who want to sexualize the next generation to their way of thinking. This is all achieved through "anti-discrimination" laws, like the one mentioned here: SB 777.

This article sadly illustrates the practical outcomes brought about by the homosexual lobby and reinforces the fact that we cannot afford to ignore this issue, because it will not conveniently go away. In other parts of the world, such as South Africa, constitutional provisions or amendments are well in place for something on the scale of SB 777 to be implemented in the schools there. It is just a matter of time. The pro-gay forces are tenacious to the end. Therefore, the church of Jesus Christ cannot afford to sit this one out.

The article is used with permission by WorldNetDaily.com.

"Mom," "dad," targeted by California bias ban: "Parents want fundamentals, not indoctrination about sex"

BY BOB UNRUH, WORLDNETDAILY.COM, SEPTEMBER 12, 2007

A new plan approved by the California Legislature could be used to ban the words "dad" or "mom" in all public schools as being discriminatory against "partner 1" and "partner 2" in same-sex relationships, according to critics.

The legislation, in fact, seeks to impose a "radical homosexual indoctrination" on the young children in the state, according to Karen

England, executive director of Capitol Resource Family Impact, a new affiliate of Capitol Resource Institute.

"It is simply outrageous that the California legislature continues to ignore the values and beliefs of citizens by forcing this radical homosexual indoctrination on our young children," England said.

The plan, SB 777, has passed the state Assembly on a 43–23 vote and it now moves forward to Gov. Arnold Schwarzenegger, who previously vetoed another similar plan, SB 1437 from 2006.

At that time, Schwarzenegger said adequate legal protections against discrimination already existed.

It bans any teaching or activities in schools that "promotes a discriminatory bias against" homosexuals, transgenders, bisexuals, and those with gender (perceived or actual) issues. England said the essence of SB 777 is that it seeks to *normalize* alternative lifestyles in California schools with special recognition for homosexuality, bisexuality, and transsexuality.

Meredith Turney, the legislative liaison for the CRFI, said a clear picture of what will be demanded of schools in the state can be obtained by looking at the Los Angeles Unified School District, which already has adopted many of the requirements being set up for statewide use now.

"LAUSD policy instructs schools to provide access to restroom and locker room facilities that 'corresponds to the gender identity that the student consistently asserts at school.' If a male student 'consistently asserts' himself as a female at school, he will be granted access to female restrooms and locker rooms. This poses a serious danger to the safety of young female students," Turney said.

"SB 777 will implement statewide the shocking policies LAUSD already enforces. Concerned parents do not want such radical, perplexing policies in their local schools. Parents want the assurance that when their children go to school they will learn the fundamentals of reading, writing and arithmetic—not social indoctrination regarding alternative sexual lifestyles," she said.

"SB 777 also will do away with such 'arcane' terms as 'mom and dad' and 'husband and wife,'" stated England. "'Promoting a discriminatory bias' is so vague that it could be interpreted to mean that any reference to traditional families is discriminatory and requires equal time for radical sexual behavior."

The Los Angeles District policy notes under its "Issues of Privacy" requirements "school personnel should not disclose a student's transgender status to others, including parents, and/or other school personnel, unless there is a specific 'need to know.'"

"Whenever discussing a particular issue such as conduct, discipline, grades, attendance, or health with a transgender or gender nonconforming student, focus on the conduct or particular issue, and not on any assumptions regarding the student's actual or perceived gender identity," the rules require. "When school personnel must contact the parents of a transgender or gender nonconforming student, 'best practice' would dictate that the student should be consulted first to determine an appropriate way to reference the student's gender identity."

Students also should be asked how they want to be addressed.

"In cases where students and parents may be in disagreement about the name and pronoun to be used at school, school officials may refer families to appropriate outside counseling services," the rules require.

CRFI noted three members of the assembly stood in opposition to the plan: Ted Gaines, Bob Huff and Chuck DeVore.

"Assemblyman Gaines expressed his concern that the bill would silence students with traditional values while Assemblyman Huff explained that the education code already protects all students—including homosexuals—from discrimination and 'harassment,'" the organization said. "Assemblyman DeVore inquired of the bill's floor manager, Assemblyman John Laird, why the bill was necessary. When Laird declared that homosexual students are discriminated against, DeVore asked for specific examples ... Laird could not share any."

"We hope that Gov. Schwarzenegger will ... [veto] this legislation that pushes a radical social agenda."

Randy Thomasson, of the Campaign for Children and Families, said the idea is just wrong.

"SB 777 requires textbooks, instructional materials and school-sponsored activities to positively portray cross-dressing, sex-change operations, homosexual 'marriages' and all aspects of homosexuality and bisexuality, including so-called 'gay history,'" he said. "Silence on these sexual lifestyles will not be allowed."

Thomasson said the notion "of forcing children to support controversial sexual lifestyles is shocking and appalling to millions of fathers and mothers."

"Parents don't want their children taught to become homosexual or bisexual or to wonder whether they need a sex-change operation. SB 777 will shatter the academic purpose of education by turning every government school into a sexual indoctrination center," he said.

The current education code's definition of "sex," which reads, "'Sex' means the biological condition or quality of being a male or female human being," is eliminated. The new "gender" definition considers "a person's gender identity and gender related appearance and behavior whether or not stereotypically associated with the person's assigned sex at birth."

The new mandate would be enforced by the attorneys of the California Department of Education, which would sue school districts that don't comply, Thomasson noted.

England earlier warned of the ramifications nationwide, including a tailoring of textbooks by publishers to meet new censorship requirements in California, the largest purchaser of textbooks in the nation.

No matter how traditional a community may be, school officials would find themselves faced with the same religious, moral and social biases instituted in California reflected in their textbooks, she warned.

As WND reported, a board member for the homosexual advocacy group Equality California verbally attacked and threatened CRI for its opposition to the bill earlier.

The board member sent an e-mail and video to CRI threatening the group would be buried if it continued efforts opposing the homosexual advocacy.

"The shocking hate mail we received shows that those behind this legislation do not promote true tolerance," said England. "Only politically correct speech will be tolerated. Those with religious or traditional moral beliefs will not be allowed to express their opinions in public schools."

She also cited an informational document published by the Gay–

Straight Alliance Network and the Transgender Law Center that already is lobbying for special treatment in the school system.

"If you want to use a restroom that matches your gender identity … you should be allowed to do so," it advises. "Whenever students are divided up into boys and girls, you should be allowed to join the group or participate in the program that matches your gender identity as much as possible."

Further, the groups advise, "If you change your name to one that better matches your gender identity, a school needs to use that name to refer to you."

WND has documented a number of earlier cases in which educators, including leaders in California, have taken it upon themselves to promote a homosexual lifestyle to children under their charge.

WND reported California Superintendent of Public Instruction Jack O'Connell, under whose supervision hundreds of thousands of children are being educated, has used his state position and taxpayer-funded stationery to praise a "gay" pride event used in the past to expose children to sexually explicit activities.

That drew vehement objections from several educators, including Priscilla Schreiber, president of the Grossmont Unified High School District governing board.

"I am outraged that a person in this high-ranking elected position would advocate an event where diversity is not just being celebrated but where pornography and indecent exposure is being perpetrated on the young and innocent children of our communities," she said.

WND also covered the issue when officials in Boulder, Colo., held a seminar for students in which they were told to "have sex," including same-sex experiences, and "take drugs."

Another school event promoted homosexuality to students while banning parents, and at still another, WND reported school officials ordered their 14-year-old freshman class into a "gay" indoctrination seminar after having them sign a confidentiality agreement promising not to tell their parents.

[This article, along with follow up articles, can be found at: worldnetdaily.com/news/article.asp?ARTICLE_ID=57593]

Appendix 2. Questions and answers

Here are just a few examples of the kinds of questions I am frequently asked regarding the issue of same-sex marriage and homosexuality.

1. Given the cultural redefining of marriage, what is a good Christian definition of marriage?

With the relativistic nature of marriage in our postmodern culture, traditional definitions have been blurred and confused. But the touchstone of Scripture has not changed and does not lend itself to the opaque meanings that have become commonplace.

A Christian definition of marriage, out of necessity, rightly finds its source in Genesis 1 and 2 in the creation mandate. Armed with this knowledge, John Stott has eloquently defined marriage as follows: "Marriage is an exclusive heterosexual covenant between one man and one woman, ordained and sealed by God, preceded by a public leaving of parents, consummated in sexual union, issuing in a permanent mutually supportive partnership, and normally crowned by the gift of children."[1] This multifaceted definition indicates that marriage is far more than just civil agreement between two people. On the contrary, marriage is first by divine design. It is duly instituted by God and finds its origin in divine sovereignty as opposed to the state's sovereignty. The state merely recognizes what God has ordained and ordered. This implies a sacredness that outweighs, but does not omit, the secular sanction.

If Western governments held to the definition given above, this book would not need to be written. If most couples getting married had a mature understanding of this definition of marriage, divorce rates would plummet and single-parent and broken homes would be few and far between!

2. We often hear that marriage is a covenant. What does that mean?

The Bible itself refers to marriage as a "covenant":

- "... to deliver you from the strange woman, from the adulteress who flatters with her words; that leaves the companion of her youth and forgets the covenant of her God" (Prov. 2:16–17).
- "Yet you say, 'For what reason?' Because the LORD has been a witness between you and the wife of your youth, against whom you have dealt treacherously, though she is your companion and your wife by covenant" (Mal. 2:14).

To say that marriage is a covenant distinguishes it from a mere civil contract, which more closely resembles a modern business contract devoid of all spiritual and moral significance—elements we normally attribute to marriage.

As a covenant, marriage is a trilateral contract before the man and God, before the woman and God, and mutually between the man and the woman. This triad results in a sacred bond between the three parties. Even when not humanly acknowledged, a marriage always involves three persons: God, the man, and the woman.[2]

Genesis 2:22–24 is written in covenantal language and is a good basis for illustrating marriage as a covenant.

The LORD God fashioned into a woman the rib which He had taken from the man, and brought her to the man. The man said,

"This is now bone of my bones,
And flesh of my flesh;
She shall be called Woman,
Because she was taken out of Man."

For this reason a man shall leave his father and his mother, and shall be joined to his wife; and they shall become one flesh.

In a marriage covenant, the man and woman solemnly pledge to an enduring commitment to each other before God as primary witness. In addition, the covenanting couple verbally and publicly guarantee that the promises and obligations made before God and man are binding until death.

Andreas Kostenberger nicely summarizes the implications of the marriage covenant, which include permanence, sacredness, intimacy, and exclusiveness (monogamy).[3] SSM can never approximate this covenant arrangement because it does not meet the divinely designated requirements of a man and a woman; it violates the basic heterosexual requirement. God's standard remains consistent throughout Scripture. The Bible relentlessly and universally condemns homosexual unions and any other union that violates the essence of the covenant God ordained from the beginning.

When the significance of marriage in the creation order is flagrantly ignored, marriage is reduced to a mere civil transaction for the purpose of a few state benefits. This is exactly what a civil union is—a civil contract for the purpose of state benefits. This opens up the door to a variety of possible marriage arrangements to include SSM, polygamy, polyamory, endogamy, and pedogamy. Such arrangements will never meet God's covenant requirements. Therefore, I do not believe that God recognizes same-sex marriages as marriages; rather, as John Piper says, SSM is state-sanctioned "fraternity."

3. What should the state's role in marriage be?
This question is much easier to ask than it is to answer. From a Christian perspective, God has ordained government for the benefit of his creation (Gen. 9:1–17; Rom. 13:1–7; 1 Peter 2:13–17). In light of this God-ordained status, what role should the state play in marriage?

A variety of opinions and answers are offered. There are libertarians who reject the notion of any government interference at all. Then the pendulum swings back to the other extreme of over-regulation.

Since I am venturing into territory that is quite out of the realm of my knowledge, I can only offer a few humble opinions based on a more nuanced theological vantage point.

The most important consideration in endeavoring to answer this query is that it depends on how the state defines marriage. For example, the new

South African constitution, in the Bill of Rights, declares that no person shall be discriminated against based on his or her "sexual orientation." This was challenged at the constitutional court level by two lesbians who wanted to marry and produced the full fruit of same-sex marriage, which became the law of the land in December 2006. Once parliament changed the marriage act from reading that marriage should be between "a man and a woman" to "between two persons," the definition was irrevocably changed.

In the USA, because of the strong Judeo-Christian influence, it has always been assumed that marriage is an exclusive heterosexual union between a man and a woman. For this reason, Utah, with its polygamy, was not allowed to become a state until it renounced polygamy. The founding fathers could never have anticipated the current challenges to marriage in the USA. As a result, marriage was never explicitly mentioned in the constitution. Now, apart from a constitutional amendment, which is quite unlikely in a Democrat-controlled White House, the definition of marriage is going to be radically revised one state at a time. Massachusetts was the first bride to this ball in 2003.

I would argue that, in a postmodern, pluralistic world, most Western governments are not going to concede to a Christian definition of marriage like the one cited by John Stott earlier. But this should not stop the Christian community from making a well-reasoned and impassioned appeal to the secular authorities that marriage is an exclusively heterosexual union between a man and a woman.

Considering that the state is ordained by God, it does have a responsibility in administrating marriage. But since marriage is also ordained by God, the state serves to *recognize* marriage, not *create* marriage. Currently, most governments are not about to acknowledge God's external authority. This is producing the matrimonial paradigm shift we are now witnessing.

So how do Christians argue for a traditional definition of marriage in completely secular states? Nobody said it would be easy! We must certainly argue the moral reason and principles from a biblical position. Additionally, as Peter Sprigg argues, there are some clear observations that can be made based on natural law: "The definition of marriage is rooted in the immutable and empirical facts of nature with respect to human reproduction."[4]

Accordingly, civil authorities should recognize their divinely ordained limits regarding the definition for marriage. Marriage is a natural institution with ample testimony from both Scripture and nature. Ignoring the patently obvious has resulted in the matrimonial revisionism that is now in vogue.

Interestingly, as recently as 1987, US Supreme Court justice Sandra Day O'Conner affirmed that marriage is "an exercise of religious faith as well as an expression of personal dedication."[5] This underscores the spiritual and moral ramifications of marriage, which lends further credence to a traditional view of marriage.

There are numerous reasons why the state has a God-given role in marriage. The state plays a vital role in administration, regulation, and protecting marriage from abuses such as the marrying of near relatives or of those who are too young. In divorce cases, the state usually seeks the best interests of the child(ren) involved.[6]

Marriage provides a wonderful benefit package for society, as Sprigg well notes: "Society gives benefits to marriage because marriage gives benefits to society."[7] The numerous benefits of marriage are well documented; marriages lead to healthier, more balanced, more stable, and more prosperous nations. Understandably, then, governments the world over offer benefits such as tax breaks, health-care supplements, and eligibility for a multitude of state-sponsored perks for families. This is one of the reasons why those outside the traditionally prescribed meaning for marriage now want to be included. The question is, are the state benefits offered to those who marry rights or privileges?

Ultimately, it is in the best interests of government to define marriage as an exclusive heterosexual union between a man and a woman. All civil administration, regulation, and state benefits accorded to marriage should flow from a traditional definition. But what the state should do and actually does do are often poles apart. It is, therefore, the believer's duty to remind government of its God-given duty. We should not be afraid to make well-reasoned appeals to those who govern our respective nations and states. If Christians do not remind the world and the secular state about the vital importance and narrow meaning of marriage, who will?

Once the state believes it has the authority to *create* marriage, you end up with the relativistic mess we have now. We have set sail on uncharted matrimonial seas and defied God in the process. It remains to be seen where this voyage will end. Of this I am certain: God will not be mocked.

4. How should we respond to a loved one or close friend who comes out of the closet and declares he or she is a homosexual?

This is a question that has come up many times since I began researching and speaking on this topic. Two years ago, I spoke on SSM in my sending church, Community Bible Church in Vallejo, California. When I finished speaking, a number of people waited to talk to me and ask this very question. Because Vallejo is in the homosexual stronghold of the San Francisco Bay area, there were many in that audience who had personally confronted this very dilemma.

So how, as Christians, should we respond? Our response should always be a redemptive response, which will include the two coordinating elements of truth and grace. There must be a healthy balance of both these spiritual commodities. An imbalance here will result in an inappropriate and lopsided response that can either unnecessarily jeopardize the relationship we have with the person, or run the risk of tarnishing our witness and testimony for Christ.

In order to guide us in responding redemptively, here are some things to recognize and guard against:

a) Recognize that there are no guarantees; this can happen to anyone, especially in this day and age. My wife's family was confronted with this very situation when someone outside her immediate family declared she was a lesbian. As time marches on, more and more Christians will come face to face with this situation, as being homosexual has become fashionable in Western culture. As more young people succumb to the cultural indoctrination, we will see the percentages of professing gays rise.

b) Guard against buying the whole "orientation" bag. It amazes me how many Christians will quickly side completely with the friend or loved one based on the argument of biological determinism. This response ignores the truth and ultimately does nothing to point the loved one in the right direction. It amounts to compromising for the sake of peace and thereby elevates pseudo-science above the Word of God. Even if science does find some kind of biological link, this should not surprise us, as we do live in a fallen world and the genome is under the effects of the curse. This will not negate God's Word on the subject.

c) Recognize that there is no adequate way to prepare for this news. This means it will produce emotional shock that often mimics the shock experienced by those who have lost a loved one. Though there may be a whole gamut of emotional swings, there are three primary responses often experienced. These three emotions could be called the GAG reflex:

- *Guilt*. The response is often one of taking ownership of the other person's sin by blaming oneself. Parents will often ask themselves, "What did I do?" or the corresponding question, "What could I have done differently?" It may be right to ask these questions, but ultimately, adults make their own decisions and are responsible before God for the lives they live. This is not the time to beat yourself up.

- *Anger*. This is a common response from fathers whose sons have come out of the closet. Often a dad will completely reject his gay son and find it near impossible to talk to him. Thoughts of "How could you do this to me and our family?" are common. This leads to "What will others think of us?" or "What will the church say?" Certainly, God's grace is needed to avoid the damaging effects of anger. Often, outside help from others, such as a pastor, is needed to help you think straight before the relationship is irreparably damaged.

- *Grief*. This is an expected and healthy response, as with the loss of a loved one. During moments of grief there may be a sense of sadness before God. You may try to avoid friends and other family members. This is normal, but do not use it as an excuse to give up on life and your other vital relationships, which are crucial to your coping with the disappointment. As a Christian, living on Exile Island is not a viable option!

d) Recognize how to deal with guilt, anger, and grief effectively. Learn to accept the situation without approving the sin. Stare reality in the face while acknowledging your vast limitations in changing the situation to your way of thinking. This means relinquishing your loved one to God and his sovereignty without abandoning him or her. Be willing to seek godly help and counsel. You need the spiritual encouragement a good biblical counselor can offer. To this end, refuse to suffer in silence.

e) Recognize that, in the uncovering of one sin, you might uncover another sin. Sixty per cent of all lesbians are reported to have been abused, molested, or raped by a close friend or family member. Many male homosexuals were molested by someone close to them, either a family member, friend of the family, or an authority figure. So prepare for the avalanche of more bad news.

f) Recognize that declarations of homosexuality can be accompanied by other disheartening news, such as "I am HIV positive."

g) Resist the temptation to retreat from the issue when someone you know declares that he or she is gay.

h) Recognize that the root of any addiction is idolatry. Misplaced worship will ultimately produce the wrong behavior. The human heart is idol factory and the mind can become a conveyor belt for sexual idolatry. As John MacArthur explains of Romans 1:18–32, "When man forsakes the Author of nature, he inevitably forsakes the order of nature."[8] Homosexuality certainly contravenes the order of creation. Hence it is the fruit of idolatry.

i) Recognize that you walk a fine line between telling the truth and doing so in love. What does a balance between the two look like in practice?

- Verse 22 of Jude says, "And have mercy on some, who are doubting." Our zeal against the sin of homosexuality needs to be tempered with mercy for the person whose salvation we seek.
- A homosexual must be told that you love him or her, but at the same time you cannot condone or support his or her sin in any way. In the case of families and parents, you must agree on a unified strategy of approaching your loved one in such a way that other relationships in the family are not imperiled or strained by working at cross purposes with each other.
- You will need to establish acceptable boundaries in the relationship. Things have drastically changed, which means the rules for

engagement in this relationship have changed as well. For instance, you cannot allow any same-sex activity to take place in your home. To do so would be to condone the sin. You need to determine what is permissible and what is not; when you should meet your loved one, where to meet, and for what duration. All of these things become huge issues that serve to further divide families and compound the heartache.

- Work on keeping the lines of communication open. In the end, let your loved one be the one to reject you, not the other way around. Homosexuals want us to accept them as they are; they must be prepared to do the same for us. A little outline I learned from biblical counselor Dr. John Street is very helpful in showing us how to keep the lines of communication open: Be honest (Eph. 4:25); keep current (Eph. 4:26); attack the problem and not the person (Eph. 4:29–30); act, don't react (be proactive, not reactive; Eph. 4:31–32). Remind yourself that there is more to your loved one than his or her homosexuality.

j) Recognize you cannot change your loved one, but with God's help you can control your responses.

k) Guard your heart by beginning a long-term ministry of prayer while seeking to encourage others in a similar situation (2 Cor. 1:3–11).[9]

5. Aren't homosexuality and SSM private matters which are nobody else's business?

This is a common rejoinder by those who are seeking to be more "tolerant" and "understanding" of the situation. The problem with this thinking is that gay-rights activists, the media, academic elites, and politicians favoring pro-gay legislation have made it everyone's business because of their in-your-face promotion of homosexuality.

It is of interest to note that ancient Israel did not have any laws of "mutual adult consent." Leviticus illustrates this well. In Leviticus 18, the term used to describe male-pursuing-male homosexuality is *zakar* (18:22), which incorporates and includes all ages of the male gender. In other words, the prohibition covers any male of any age engaging in homosexual acts. Likewise, the women of all ages (*neqeba*) in Leviticus 18 are protected and commanded to observe divinely prescribed sexual boundaries. There are no age limits or loopholes available here. The idea of two consenting adults privately violating God's laws regarding sexuality is foreign. Regardless of what two adults may consent to behind closed doors, God's borders remain, as what happens in private affects the whole nation.

The presumption today is that two or more individuals can carry out whatever private desires they have without affecting or influencing society in any way. The Bible clearly debunks this selfish and hyper-individualistic notion. The world is today creaking under the weight of sins committed in private that are assumed to be nobody else's business.

The family may break down in private, but the repercussions ripple through all of society in a thousand different ways. Every man doing that which is right in his own eyes will produce the fracture and fragmentation of society every time, regardless of perceived cultural advances. Therefore, it is right to point out that what is done in private often has a very public price tag attached to it. Maybe this, in part, is why Leviticus 19:18 declares, "you shall love your neighbor as yourself"!

6. Did Jesus advocate homosexuality?

The prevailing SSM opinion is that silence on the part of Jesus concerning homosexuality is golden. SSM interpreters argue that, since Jesus did not explicitly single out homosexuality with some defining statement, homosexuality is therefore no longer taboo. But the silence of Jesus on this matter needs to be considered in light of what we do know. Here are a few defining considerations about Jesus based on what is known. These shed an incriminating light on the stock SSM argument from silence.

- Jesus was an active agent in the act of creation itself (Col. 1:15–17). As creator, Jesus came to fulfill the creation order, which the first Adam squandered. He did not come to violate creation order, which would be the case had he endorsed homosexuality or any other sexual sin. Jesus came in keeping with the order he helped establish in the beginning (Gen. 1 and 2).
- Rather than abolishing the Law—which includes Leviticus 18:22 and 20:13—Jesus came to perfectly fulfill the Law (Matt. 5:17–19). The whole of the Law is now reinterpreted and filtered through the divine

person and finished work of Christ upon the cross. That Christ fulfilled the dictates and demands of the Law does not nullify the moral principles derived from it. On judgment day, unbelievers will be judged in accordance with the Law's just demands (Rev. 21:8).

- There are many sins that Christ never mentioned or focused upon. Rather than concentrating on specific acts of sin, Jesus focused on the nature and origin of sin: the heart of man. He taught that, because man is constitutionally a sinner by nature, individual acts of sin are the external result—whatever those individual acts of sin may be. Note the emphasis Jesus placed on the internal condition of man:

... there is nothing outside the man which can defile him if it goes into him; but the things which proceed out of the man are what defile the man. (Mark 7:15)

But the things that proceed out of the mouth come from the heart, and those defile the man. For out of the heart come evil thoughts, murders, *adulteries*, *fornications*, thefts, false witness, slanders. These are the things which defile the man; but to eat with unwashed hands does not defile the man. (Matt. 15:18–20, emphasis added)

In other words, homosexuality is one of a multitude of expressions of the sin nature. So rather than listing thousands of sins by name and filling up volumes of books doing so, Jesus dealt with the root of these external acts of sin. That Jesus mentioned "adulteries" and "fornications" covers the wide array of sexual sins that violate the seventh commandment. Just because Jesus did not mention a specific sin by name, it does not mean that it is acceptable in God's eyes. Clearly, Jesus placed a significant emphasis on the internal matters of the heart.

- As a result of Christ's first advent, the OT Law took on universal dimensions as it was applied to the Gentile nations through the new-covenant provisions of redemption found in Christ. Christians are therefore to love God and then their neighbors as themselves, which, given the extreme demands of this, is ultimately an impossibility apart from both saving and enabling grace. The whole purpose of Christ's coming was to do what the Law could not do—to save (Mark 10:45; Luke 19:10). The Law of God is a schoolmaster that shows sinners their need for Christ. The Law only makes the diagnosis of sin. Christ is the only prescription for that sin!

- Jesus upheld and reaffirmed the creation mandate of gender distinction and marriage when he was questioned about divorce and remarriage (Matt. 19:4–6; Mark 10:2–11). He regarded the creation male–female requirement for marriage as an absolute necessity. He did not alter or amend the Genesis 1 and 2 ideal one bit. He underscored it, along with the two cardinal principles of monogamy and a lifelong commitment.

- When Jesus made that marriage/divorce pronouncement, he said all that ever needed to be said. As earlier noted, he did not speak out on other sexual sins, such as incest, bestiality, or polygamy, but he did not need to when he reasserted the creation mandate. Jesus's statement on marriage was a one-size-fits-all ruling on all sexual deviations that depart from the marriage ideal.

So, did Jesus condone homosexuality? The SSM advocate is very hard-pressed to substantiate that such was the case. If he condoned homosexuality, we might conclude that he also condoned bestiality, necrophilia, and incest. After all, he never uttered a word about these things either.

7. How do the passages in Leviticus on homosexuality (18:22; 20:13) square with New Testament teaching?

There are two extremes where the issue of the Law in the NT is concerned. The first recklessly claims that we are freed from the Law through Christ. Therefore, the OT Law has absolutely no place in the life of twenty-first-century believers, because we are saved by grace, not Law. The opposite extreme seeks to apply all of the civil and moral aspects of the OT legislation to our current NT setting in the church. So how should we navigate between these positions?

It must be remembered that the Bible is progressive revelation that traces the development and change from God dealing with Israel as a nation to God dealing with the church (Jews and Gentiles alike) as the Bride of Christ. This progressive nature of Scripture allows for the function and form of the OT Law to change as God's plan for redemption unfolds throughout the pages of the Bible. The Law has always been a mirror to point out the sinfulness of humanity in every age. It illustrates just how far short of the glory of God man is apart from Jesus Christ. Moreover, it points the sinner to Christ and his redeeming love. But once saved, the believer is not off the hook and free to live any way he or she pleases. The new-covenant believer is not free from the Law, but is now bound to the law of Christ, who fulfilled the just demands of the Law on the cross.

SSM logic assumes that passages like Leviticus 18:22 and 20:13 are just as irrelevant as dietary laws and the mixing of fabrics. Yet Romans 10:4 declares that "Christ is the end of the law." This means Christ was the crescendo of the Law. He did not come to abolish the Law, but to fulfill it. In view of his finished work on the cross, Christ is now superimposed over the Mosaic Law and has transformed it into the law of Christ (Gal. 6:2).

So the Law remains an authoritative part of Scripture. But it must now be read through the lens of the cross. For example, we do not need animal sacrifice in order to stand in the presence of God, but we do need sacrifice—the sacrifice of Christ. Likewise, the husband who loves his wife as Christ does the church will duly consider his menstruating wife's needs and condition above and beyond his own (Lev. 20:18).

The law of Christ ensures that moral unity exists between the OT and NT. It has always been wrong to murder, rape, steal, to have sexual relations with an animal, to commit adultery, and to commit homosexual acts. God's standard of righteousness has never been altered, but these righteous demands were met by Christ.

So Law is not orphaned in the NT, but rather is transformed through Christ. The NT believer, therefore, though not saved by the Law, is now to be obedient to the law of Christ, which includes the same sexual proscriptions established since the beginning. The Law has morphed beyond dietary laws and the sowing of two kinds of seed together. Rather than abandoning the Law completely, the church of Christ applies it differently from how the nation of Israel applied it in OT times. Yet it is clear that the sexual prohibitions of the OT are still applicable today.

But SSM interpreters like Lilly Nortje-Meyer still stubbornly claim,

Paul declared in no uncertain terms that Christ was the end of the torah (Rom. 10:4)

and therefore Paul exempted the gentile Christians from keeping the torah. It is only the sexual laws that he sustained and applied vigorously. The Church sustained this point of view unchanged for two thousand years and condemned people who placed their hope and faith in God to a living hell ... The Church did not practice the message of inclusivity that lies at the heart of the Bible transcending the culturally bound messages that marginalize women, slaves and homosexual people.[10]

Nortje-Meyer's attempt to sanction homosexuality falls flat on many fronts. Her glib approach to the Law is a feeble attempt to dismiss the Law entirely so she can validate an antinomian (lawless) viewpoint. She apparently is totally unaware that, where sin is concerned, God is exclusive in his holy character, not inclusive. The Bible never transcends sexual sin of any nature. Otherwise Christ died in vain and justice is not served.

8. But isn't holding to the traditional view of homosexuality the same as promoting slavery, suppressing women, and endorsing apartheid?

The thinking is that, in the past, the church was wrong about these things, so it stands to reason that we are wrong about homosexuality today. But these are all very poor analogies. This logic amounts to apples and oranges theology. There simply is not a one-to-one correspondence when comparing homosexuality with these other three issues. Not all analogies are equal, nor do they all carry the same weight.

A) WHY IS LIKENING HOMOSEXUALITY TO SLAVERY A BAD COMPARISON?

- There is absolutely no mandate or precedent in the Bible that commands us to enslave other people. Contrast this with the straightforward proscriptions against homosexuality throughout the Bible, in both the OT and the NT.
- The heterosexual norm for marriage was established in a pre-Fall world; slavery is a post-Fall consequence of sin.
- At the time the OT laws were issued, slavery was pervasive in the ancient world. In response to this all-too-common reality, the Bible sought to regulate and govern slavery, introducing kindness and compassionate treatment for those who were slaves in the Hebrew

economy, which, according to scholars, actually had far fewer slaves than the rest of the world. But on those occasions when it was a matter of starve or become a slave, passages like Exodus 21:2–11 and Leviticus 25:39 outlined the terms for one Hebrew owning another Hebrew: "And if a countryman of yours becomes so poor with regard to you that he sells himself to you, you shall not subject him to a slave's service" (Lev. 25:39).

- It is helpful to remember that the slavery the Bible regulated for Israel was very different from the slavery of the modern era. For starters, biblical regulations for Israel were never racially motivated. Instead, it was sometimes an economic necessity in a world that was devoid of any form of national welfare programs for the poor and disadvantaged. Many slaves earned a salary, many were educated and held positions of great responsibility, such as being stewards over the master's domain. In some instances, a slave could buy his or her way out of slavery. That is not to say there weren't abuses.

- In the NT, Paul indicates that, if a slave has the opportunity to get freedom from slavery, it should be pursued: "Were you called while a slave? Do not worry about it; but if you are able also to become free, rather do that. For he who was called in the Lord while a slave, is the Lord's freedman; likewise he who was called while free, is Christ's slave. You were bought with a price; do not become slaves of men" (1 Cor. 7:21–23).

- It was William Wilberforce, a Christian, who led the charge for the abolition of the slave trade in the early 1800s. Based on biblical principles, Wilberforce was eventually successful in promoting the abolition of the slave trade in Great Britain.

- While the Bible never condemns slavery, it never commands it, either. God sovereignly chose to govern slavery humanely for his chosen people Israel. Unlike slavery, the Bible never seeks to regulate or govern homosexuality any more than it seeks to regulate other sexual vices. The NT believer is never called upon to practice or govern slavery, but is warned to flee homosexuality.

B) ISN'T THE OPPRESSIVE TREATMENT OF WOMEN AS THE INFERIOR GENDER IN THE MODERN WEST THE EQUIVALENT OF THE MODERN CHURCH'S TREATMENT OF HOMOSEXUALS?

- Scripture does not teach that gender is mutable and transformative. But sexual orientation is.
- Being a woman is never viewed as sinful in the Bible, unlike homosexuality. There are no divine pronouncements of judgment for being a woman.
- The Bible indicates that there is an equality of essence that women have with men, but the divinely ordained roles for women are distinct from those of men.
- Galatians 3:28 details the level playing that all have in light of the cross of Christ: "There is neither Jew nor Greek, there is neither slave nor free man, there is neither male nor female; for you are all one in Christ Jesus." This is not meant to eradicate gender distinctions and affirm same-sex attraction. On the contrary, this verse relates to salvation and being a new creature in Christ. There is no advantage based on ethnicity, class, or gender. Salvation is equally available for all. Christianity is not like some secret society in which ethnicity, class, or gender might become a determining factor for acceptance.
- The biblical view actually affirms women. Compared with the surrounding cultures of the time in which it was written, the Bible provided a much greater degree of dignity and respect for women. In this, women in the biblical worldview found their freedom and fulfillment.[11]
- The Bible contains numerous positive portrayals of women in stark contrast to the consistent negative portrayal of homosexuality throughout both the OT and the NT. Homosexual activity is always treated as a gross violation of God's sexual ethics in Scripture. There is absolutely no biblical ambiguity on the subject.
- Therefore the Bible uniformly promotes the kind and equitable treatment of women. To treat women as inferior is always contrary to Scripture, while the firm denunciation of homosexuality is consistent right through God's Word.

C) ISN'T THE COMPARISON BETWEEN APARTHEID[12] AND HOMOSEXUALITY AN APPROPRIATE ONE?

- Again, this is a mismatched comparison. Apartheid was legislated racism that found its impetus more in a subjective interpretation of the Scripture than in solid exegesis. In the Great Trek (in the 1830s), the early Voortrekkers (Afrikaner pioneers in South Africa) subjectively read their experiences and encounters with the various African tribes into the Bible. They saw themselves as the new Israel in the land of promise. Instead of Canaanites and Jebusites, the Voortrekkers had Zulus and Xhosas to contend with. This misreading of Scripture paved the way for legislative apartheid 120 years later.

- God did not expel the Canaanites from the Promised Land because of race, but because of the curse of Canaan for the unchecked sin of the Canaanites.

- The Bible is quite clear on the issue of racism and discrimination. Jesus said to the Jews, "I have other sheep, which are not of this fold" (John 10:16). Colossians 3:10–11 and Ephesians 2:11–21 are clear reminders that God has made of all nations one blood. That some churches blatantly disregarded such verses is an indictment against them. No person is eternally judged by God because of his or her race. The new-covenant provisions of redemption through and in Christ are available to all without distinction, but repentance from sin is required to appropriate these provisions of saving grace. The person who professes repentance while clutching to cherished sins like adultery, fornication, drunkenness, or homosexuality has not truly repented.

- Apartheid is another example of the consequences of the Fall and the entrance of sin into the world. The promotion of such prejudice owes more to the influence of evolutionary thinking than to the Bible. The intentional misinterpretation of the Bible became a convenient way authoritatively to promote apartheid's racist-driven agenda.

- As with gender, race is not a mutable condition, nor is it sinful. Race is inviolable and immutable. A person is permanently consigned to whichever race he or she is born. Race is certain and fixed, while homosexual orientation is not. I have never met a former Caucasian or a former African, but I have met former homosexuals who, by grace, have been liberated from the shackles of what the Bible calls a sin.

The use of analogies like those above is not a balanced or honest way to promote SSM in the church. These all fall far short of making the necessary point SSM advocates try to make. In the end, the use of such strained analogies indicates that SSM articulators are not far removed in their approach from the promoters of apartheid, who relativistically read their experiences into the pages of the Bible!

9. What is US President Barack Obama's position on gay rights and SSM?

Given that during the US presidential campaign Barack Obama claimed he did not fully support SSM, what are we to make of his position on the issue? In short, his position on gay rights and SSM is as radical and far reaching as his views on abortion, which amount to infanticide.[13] The best way to answer the question is to use the words of Obama himself from a statement he issued to the gay community:

Equality is a moral imperative. That's why throughout my career, I have fought to eliminate discrimination against LGBT Americans. In Illinois, I co-sponsored a fully inclusive bill that prohibited discrimination on the basis of both sexual orientation and gender identity, extending protection to the workplace, housing, and places of public accommodation. In the US Senate, I have co-sponsored bills that would equalize tax treatment for same-sex couples and provide benefits to domestic partners of federal employees. And as president, I will place the weight of my administration behind the enactment of the Matthew Shepard Act to outlaw hate crimes and a fully inclusive Employment Non-Discrimination Act to outlaw workplace discrimination on the basis of sexual orientation and gender identity [emphasis added].[14]

The first sentence says it all: "Equality is a moral imperative." It is basically all downhill from there. Though he may have tried to distance himself from gay marriage during the campaign, it is evident that was only because it was politically expedient for him to do so. He has no moral convictions or ethical squabbles with homosexuality or its related issues. Essentially, he will try to promote comprehensive gay-rights legislation that will irrevocably empower this tiny minority to enslave the many who deem homosexuality morally abhorrent.

Once this wide-ranging list of gay-friendly legislation is signed into law, Bible-believing Christians will be in the cross hairs of the ACLU (American Civil Liberties Union) and gay-rights crusaders, who will tar and brand all who disagree as "right-wing bigots" and "homophobes." We will see the professed "tolerance" that gay-rights sympathizers preach quickly morph into tyranny as these cultural transvaluationists begin applying hate-crime laws and hate-speech legislation to Christians and conservative congregations.

President Obama has also called for the complete repeal of the federal version of the Defense of Marriage Act (DOMA). Obama is on record saying, "... I believe we should get rid of that statute altogether. Federal law should not discriminate in any way against gay and lesbian couples, which is precisely what DOMA does. I have also called for us to repeal Don't Ask, Don't Tell ..."[15]

The federal DOMA was enacted by a Republican-led congress in 1996 to regulate matters related to tax status, immigration, and social security as it relates to SSM. As the basis of the regulation, the DOMA defines marriage as between a man and a woman. In addition, this DOMA gives all fifty states the autonomy to reject same-sex marriages from other states that performed them.[16]

By completely repealing the DOMA, Obama will jeopardize every state DOMA in the country—most states have their own individual DOMAs. This will probably require one state with a DOMA to recognize another state's same-sex marriages. For example, a state like Texas would be forced to recognize the same-sex marriages of those who were married in the state of Massachusetts, should such couples relocate to Texas.

It should not be surprising that Obama uses Scripture to advance his gay-rights panacea. In his book *The Audacity of Hope*, he staunchly contends that he relies heavily on "... the Sermon on the Mount, which I think is, in my mind, for my faith, more central than an obscure passage in Romans."[17]

Only a thorough-going postmodern-trained attorney (Harvard Law School) could make such an outrageous assertion regarding the following passage:

> Therefore God gave them over in the lusts of their hearts to impurity, so that their bodies would be dishonored among them. For they exchanged the truth of God for a lie, and worshiped and served the creature rather than the Creator, who is blessed forever. Amen. For this reason God gave them over to degrading passions; for their women exchanged the natural function for that which is unnatural, and in the same way also the men abandoned the natural function of the woman and burned in their desire toward one another, men with men committing indecent acts and receiving in their own persons the due penalty of their error. And just as they did not see fit to acknowledge God any longer, God gave them over to a depraved mind, to do those things which are not proper ... (Rom. 1:24–28)

There is absolutely nothing obtuse or opaque about Romans' graphic portrayal of homosexuality. In order to be so dismissive, a person must intentionally deny the obvious.

Obama's ignorance regarding both the Romans account and the Sermon on the Mount is glaring given the following considerations from the Sermon:

- Where in the Sermon on the Mount (Matt. 5–7) is homosexuality ever promoted or approved, even tacitly? Further, where in the Sermon on the Mount is the teaching of Romans 1:24–28 ever contravened or questioned?
- In Matthew 5:17–18, Jesus said he did not come to abolish the Law, but to fulfill it. Jesus upheld even the lesser laws like those related to tithing, so it is unreasonable to think that he abrogated the sexual ethics contained in OT Law.
- In the Sermon on the Mount, Jesus used six antitheses to expand the dictates and demands of the Law by applying it to matters of the heart (mind, will, and emotions). The sum of these antitheses was to target the thoughts and motives of any would-be follower of Christ. Two of the six antitheses relate directly to marriage and sexuality: "You have heard that it was said, 'You shall not commit adultery'; but I say to

you, that everyone who looks at a woman with lust for her has already committed adultery with her in his heart" (Matt. 5:27–28); "It was said, 'Whoever sends his wife away, let him give her a certificate of divorce'; but I say to you that everyone who divorces his wife, except for the reason of unchastity, makes her commit adultery; and whoever marries a divorced woman commits adultery" (Matt. 5:31– 32). These two passages cover the essential terrain of the seventh and tenth commandments (adultery and covetousness).[18] If anything, Jesus was actually increasing the demands of sexual laws to include one's thought life. Not only is it a sin to commit adultery, to fornicate, to commit incest, to rape, and to perform homosexual acts; it is also a sin even to ponder such things in our hearts.

- In these two antitheses, Jesus emphasized the distinct priority of male–female union only afforded in heterosexual marriage. He never intimated that any other arrangement is acceptable. He also underscored that the nature of the heterosexual union is to be both a lifelong commitment and monogamous.

- It is true that the Sermon addresses other themes, such as loving our enemies (5:43–48) and not hypocritically judging others for small matters when much larger issues loom large in our own lives (7:1–6). "However," as Robert Gagnon concludes, "these themes provide no more support for homosexual unions than they do for loving, committed polyamorous or polygamous unions or for adult-consensual incestuous unions, both of which Jesus obviously opposed."[19]

- Given that Obama uses the Sermon on the Mount as support for his "moral imperative" for gay-rights legislation, it is interesting he says nothing of the end of that sermon, where Jesus sternly warned,

Beware of the false prophets, who come to you in sheep's clothing, but inwardly are ravenous wolves … Not everyone who says to Me, "Lord, Lord," will enter the kingdom of heaven; but he who does the will of My Father who is in heaven will enter. Many will say to Me on that day, "Lord, Lord, did we not prophesy in Your name, and in Your name cast out demons, and in Your name perform many miracles?" And then I will declare to them, "I never knew you; depart from Me, you who practice lawlessness." (Matt. 7:15)

God's will regarding sexual ethics is straightforward and obvious throughout Scripture. Jesus considers violation of the Genesis 2:22–24 mandate for marriage lawlessness, which includes homosexuality and SSM. Just because Barack Obama passes legislation favoring homosexuality, it does not make it any less lawless in God's eyes. In the end, Obama's "moral imperative" amounts to moral impudence from Christ's perspective.

Indeed, President Obama needs much prayer regarding both his views on gay rights and his eclipsed understanding of what Jesus really thinks about this issue.

10. If a person has sex-change surgery, does his or her gender really change?

I remember when a pastor friend of mine once called me to ask some questions regarding homosexuality and transsexuality.[20] In the course of our conversation, he related a situation he faced in his church with a couple, in which one of the male partners had undergone gender-reassignment surgery to become a woman. He asked me what I thought about this.

My first thought was that I was glad this was not my problem! But then I responded by simply saying that, even with all the surgery and hormone treatment, the man's basic biology was still masculine. For example, the chromosomal makeup was still XY not XX. In short—and to be blunt—this person was a mutilated male, not a woman. That meant that the marriage between the two was a same-sex marriage in God's eyes.

Transsexuality is really the pinnacle of gender-bending. Thanks to psychology and New Age religions, there is a belief that every person is a complex of male and female and that we need to somehow get in touch with both gender aspects. In many pagan religions, the person who taps into both genders and manifests androgynous tendencies is thought to be the most spiritual. In some American Indian tribes, these people become the medicine men or shamans.

In recent days, we have heard a lot about Thomas Beatie, who has been touted as the first man to become pregnant. Predictably, many people, such as Oprah Winfrey, have made Beatie out to be a hero (or heroine?) and promoted the whole erroneous notion of a pregnant man. Beatie, however, is, sadly, a mutilated female who simply has some male-like features and masculine mannerisms. This does not make a man.

All the surgery and hormone treatment in the world can only change some essential features that will help accentuate certain mannerisms of the sex a person desires to be, but medicine is powerless to change what God has made. It is God who made them male and female. All the opinions and wishful thinking to the contrary will not change this basic fact!

11. If someone makes a profession of faith in Christ but subsequently declares he or she is gay, will this person go to heaven or hell?

The answer to this question has the potential to generate a great deal of emotion. Therefore, a better way of approaching the issue is to rephrase the question. What is really at stake here is whether or not someone who is in persistent sexual sin is saved or not. While it is true that once saved, always saved, it is equally true that a legitimately saved person will desire a life of ongoing spiritual transformation and will not remain in an immoral lifestyle indefinitely.

The parable of the soils (Matt. 13:1–21; Mark 4:1–20; Luke 8:4–15) well illustrates that the seed planted in shallow ground and the seed mingled with the weeds or thorns produce no genuine or lasting fruit; such people cannot, therefore, be considered genuinely Christian. Only those who produce lasting fruit are truly saved. Someone who promotes his or her sexuality as the centerpiece of his or her faith evidences the faith of a weedy-ground hearer, which is ultimately silenced by the noxious philosophies of the world.

The five following facets of true faith help identify the sincerity of a person's profession of faith:

A) TRUE FAITH IN CHRIST IS ALWAYS ACCOMPANIED BY A CHANGED LIFE IN CHRIST

True Christian character contrasts with the character the world displays. The apostle Paul repeatedly addresses this phenomenon of a transformed life that models new behavior in keeping with Christ:

Or do you not know that the unrighteous will not inherit the kingdom of God? Do not be deceived; neither fornicators, nor idolaters, nor adulterers, nor effeminate, nor homosexuals, nor thieves, nor the covetous, nor drunkards, nor revilers, nor swindlers, will inherit the kingdom of God. Such were some of you; but you were washed, but you were sanctified, but you were justified in the name of the Lord Jesus Christ and in the Spirit of our God. (1 Cor. 6:9–11)

For the flesh sets its desire against the Spirit, and the Spirit against the flesh; for these are in opposition to one another, so that you may not do the things that you please. But if you are led by the Spirit, you are not under the Law. Now the deeds of the flesh are evident, which are: immorality, impurity, sensuality, idolatry, sorcery, enmities, strife, jealousy, outbursts of anger, disputes, dissensions, factions, envying, drunkenness, carousing, and things like these, of which I forewarn you, just as I have forewarned you, that those who practice such things will not inherit the kingdom of God. (Gal. 5:17–21)

For this you know with certainty, that no immoral [a general term for a variety of sexual sins] or impure person or covetous man, who is an idolater, has an inheritance in the kingdom of Christ and God. *Let no one deceive you with empty words*, for because of these things the wrath of God comes upon the sons of disobedience. (Eph. 5:5–6)

These verses all demonstrate that the believer's present condition in Christ should consistently clash with his or her unregenerate past. This does not imply perfection on the believer's part, but rather that the believer is no longer characterized by the old life. Paul's emphasis is "Such were some of you." The past should not intrude into the present as the two are inherently incompatible. A former drunk who is in Christ should no longer be classified as such. The same is true for homosexuals.

When the professing believer's life is dominated and defined by sins like homosexuality instead of by Christ, this is cause for concern. The weight of eternity hangs in the balance because a true believer should desire to deal with such sin rather than obstinately excusing it, as many homosexuals do. To indefinitely carry on down the same old path of sin without conviction of sin and commitment to change is damning evidence of a fraudulent faith.

B) TRUE FAITH EVIDENCES A CONSISTENT COMMITMENT TO NEW LIFE IN CHRIST
The epistle of 1 John is dedicated to the task of contrasting real faith with false faith. Genuine belief distinguishes itself by following Christ consistently enough to obey him. True faith is tenacious in its pursuit of Christ, which includes Christlike conformity:

As for you, let that abide in you which you heard from the beginning. If what you heard from the beginning abides in you, you also will abide in the Son and in the Father. (1 John 2:24)

By this we know that we love the children of God, when we love God and observe His commandments. For this is the love of God, that we keep His commandments; and His commandments are not burdensome. For whatever is born of God overcomes the world; and this is the victory that has overcome the world—our faith. Who is the one who overcomes the world, but he who believes that Jesus is the Son of God? (1 John 5:2–5)

Biblical faith goes beyond merely accepting the message of the cross. True faith commits a person to the dictates of the gospel message. True faith is radical, as the believer seeks to demonstrate professed love for Christ by obeying him. Christ should be all and in all in the believer's life. The glory of Christ trumps the fleshly desires and whims of the believer.

The rich young ruler is a good illustration of accepting or receiving the basic message of the gospel but being unwilling to radically commit himself to the personal implications of that message. Accepting the message and committing oneself to it are two entirely different matters. I am convinced there are many who accept the gospel but never commit themselves to it. This is the difference between heaven and hell.

The application is simple. When the homosexual vows allegiance to Christ yet continues to stubbornly justify and rationalize what the Bible unapologetically condemns, questions concerning the authenticity of that profession of faith are entirely legitimate. Whatever is born of God is ultimately victorious over the world and its values.

C) TRUE FAITH WILL EVIDENCE ITSELF IN SOUL-PIERCING CONVICTION OVER PERSONAL SIN

One of the common characteristics among the spiritual giants of the faith over the past 2,000 years of church history is that they were all smitten with conviction of their own personal sin. From the apostle Paul to Jonathan Edwards and C. H. Spurgeon, they all had a keen awareness of their own sinfulness.

In Paul's own testimony in 1 Timothy 1:12–17, he evidences a Romans-7 awareness of his own sin. This sensitivity to his own sinfulness allowed him to confess and forsake such sin. By acknowledging his sin, Paul was prepared to confess it. But in the pro-gay literature I have read, I have yet to come across a pro-gay theologian who talks about sin in this way. Normally, pro-gay theologians only see sin in those who dare to speak out against homosexuality.

Therefore, one of the overarching characteristics of real saving faith is a fundamental sensitivity to one's own sin. But what does this say of those who intransigently cling to sins like homosexuality? Failure to deal with such obvious sins can only produce a corresponding insensitivity to lesser and more subtle sins.

This is a vital point. True spirituality entails a spiritual sensitivity to accurately assess one's life in light of Scripture. An honest acknowledgment of life-dominating sins, including homosexuality, leads to a dedication to the necessary biblical correctives that will pave the way for life-transforming change.

D) TRUE FAITH IN CHRIST LEADS TO A RADICAL TRANSFORMATION OF THE BELIEVER'S THOUGHT LIFE

A mind transformed by God's Spirit and filled with God's Word serves as a catalyst for a significant change in behavior, as old things have passed away and all things are become new (2 Cor. 5:17). The following two verses promote a change of mind that will lead a believer to the gateway of transformed behavior:

… and that you be renewed in the spirit of your mind … (Eph. 4:23)

And do not be conformed to this world, but be transformed by the renewing of your mind, so that you may prove what the will of God is, that which is good and acceptable and perfect. (Rom. 12:2)

The key to winning the battle over any sexual sin is first to address the way such sin is entertained in the mind. The psalmist portrays this well in Psalm 119:9–11:

How can a young man keep his way pure?
    By keeping it according to Your word.
With all my heart I have sought You;
    Do not let me wander from Your commandments.
Your word I have treasured in my heart,
    That I may not sin against You.

The young man in this psalm has a mind that craves God's Word and then endeavors to apply God's Word to every situation of life. Those mired in sexual sin always have a thought life consumed by sexual thoughts and desires. The sex-saturated mind has a "no vacancy" sign for God's truth on the subject. The road to defeating sexual sin is to replace these carnal thoughts with the mind of God on the matter from the Bible.

E) TRUE FAITH IS WILLING TO PURSUE RADICAL MEASURES TO OVERCOME SEXUAL SIN

In the Sermon on the Mount, Christ made a very provocative statement regarding the rooting-out of sin in our lives. These words are most instructive and highlight the extreme measures sometimes required to slay the dragon of life-dominating sin, like homosexuality:

If your right eye makes you stumble, tear it out and throw it from you; for it is better for you to lose one of the parts of your body, than for your whole body to be thrown into hell. If your right hand makes you stumble, cut it off and throw it from you; for it is better for you to lose one of the parts of your body, than for your whole body to go into hell. (Matt. 5:29–30)

Jesus was not advocating the actual dismemberment of one's body to overcome entrenched sin. Rather, Christ was using a form of hyperbole to illustrate the necessity for the sinner to take drastic and decisive action in order to release the chokehold of sin. As with many other sins, those in the hostile grip of sexual sin or homosexuality will need to be willing to make drastic changes if emancipation from such sin is ever to be achieved.

While praying is vital—indeed, absolutely essential—to the process of radical change, prayer must be accompanied by what many might perceive as being radical correctives which will impact the whole life of the homosexual. From friends to past-times, the entire life of the homosexual is to be subject to the radical demands of change, which is all part of putting off the old man while donning the new man. An alcoholic was once counseled that living across the street from a liquor store was not a good idea. Cutting oneself off from the old life is a necessary prerequisite for victory over the nature of deep-seated sin.

While true faith is always evidenced in very tangible ways, like those listed above, this is not to imply that salvation is by works. As I am fond of telling people, we do not work *for* our salvation, we work *from* our salvation (Eph. 2:8–10). Salvation is all of God's grace, but then the believer is to work out that salvation with fear and trembling (Phil. 2:12), which is an expression of true saving grace.

In the end, it is an all-wise and sovereign God who condemns and consigns the impenitent to an eternity apart from him. At the last judgment, in Revelation 20:13, all unbelievers are judged according to their deeds (works), which ultimately testify to their unregenerate state of unbelief. These unbelievers die without an adequate covering for their sin because they refused God's gracious provision for sin through Jesus Christ. One of the categories by which the unbelieving are judged is implied in Revelation 21:8, where it refers to "immoral persons." This is a general, overarching term (*pornos*) used to implicate all those who insist on transgressing God's prescribed boundaries for human sexuality, which includes pre-marital sex, adultery, homosexuality, or any other deviancy from the Genesis 2:22–24 mandate. Refusal to repent of sexual sin is indicative of a heart of unbelief, which is subject to the wrath of God.

When the homosexual stubbornly continues in a sin God clearly condemns, the validity of his or her professed faith is surely suspect. Such persons need to heed the admonition Paul issued to the Corinthians in 2 Corinthians 13:5: "Test yourselves to see if you are in the faith; examine yourselves!" For those who sincerely acknowledge and repent from the sin of homosexuality, God promises forgiveness, freedom, and an eternal home with him, all based on the finished work of Christ on the cross and his resurrection power!

Notes

1 Quoted in **Andreas J. Kostenberger** and **David W. Jones,** *God, Marriage, and Family: Rebuilding the Biblical Foundation* (Wheaton, IL: Crossway, 2004), p. 86.

2 There are those who maintain that simply sleeping with a person means they are married. But the verses given indicate that a covenant, like the one expressed in this answer, is required for actual marriage to take place.

3 **Kostenberger and Jones,** *God, Marriage, and Family*, pp. 89–91.

4 **Sprigg,** *Outrage*, p. 10.

5 Turner v. Safely, 482 U.S. 78, 95–96, 1987.

6 Most of the papers and seminars I studied on this topic placed reproduction and the well-being of the children among the cardinal reasons for state involvement in marriage. Regulation in these areas is crucial for the vitality and stability of a nation. They are not, however, the only reasons for regulating marriage.

7 Sprigg, *Outrage*, p. 63.

8 **John MacArthur,** "God's Word on Homosexuality: The Truth about Sin and the Reality of Forgiveness," *The Master's Seminary Journal*, 19:2 (2008), p.167.

9 The information for the answer to this question was adapted from a seminar given by **John Freeman,** "When Sons and Daughters Say they are Gay." Available in MP3 format from ccef.org. Also see harvestusa.org.

10 Lilly Nortje-Meyer, "Critical Principles for a Homosexual Reading of Biblical Texts: An Introduction," *Scriptura*, 88 (2005), p. 180.

11 A recent newspaper article even supports this idea by quoting some feminist theologians who concede that the Bible extols women. See **Bess Twiston Davies,** "Is the Bible Sexist? New Research Claims Bible's Negative Stance on Women is a Myth," October 6, 2008, at timesonline.co.uk.

12 Apartheid was the political dogma to which white-ruled South Africa was subjected for the second half of the twentieth century. Simply defined, it meant the separate development of the races, but it amounted to legislated racism in South Africa.

13 As Illinois state senator, Barack Obama voted against the Born Free Act, which would allow babies born alive during abortion the chance to have access to medical care.

14 See my.barackobama.com/page/community/post/alexokrent/gGggJS, February 28, 2008.

15 Ibid.

16 The US Constitution has a "Full Faith and Credit Clause" which mandates the recognition by all states of the "acts, records, and judicial proceedings" of other states. In the case of the federal DOMA, this clause is suspended and not in force.

17 Michael Foust, "Obama: Sermon on the Mount Supports Gay Civil Unions," March 3, 2008, at bpnews.net.

18 The Ten Commandments serve as paradigmatic law, which means these laws are more extensively explained and expounded in the rest of the Law, where specific applications are given. For example, Leviticus 18 is an application of both the seventh and the tenth commands.

19 Robert Gagnon, "Barack Obama's Disturbing Misreading of the Sermon on the Mount as Support for Homosexual Sex," October 23, 2008. Also see "Obama's Coming War on Historic Christianity over Homosexual Practice and Abortion," November 2, 2008. Both articles at robgagnon.net.

20 Transsexuality differs from transvestism in that a transvestite just dresses and acts like a woman or man, whereas a transsexual has sex-change surgery followed by ongoing hormone treatments.

Appendix 3. Heads up from the headlines!

As a kid growing up, one of my favorite games in Physical Education class was a good, old-fashioned game of no-holds-barred dodgeball. I was not particularly adept at the game, but I always enjoyed the keen levels of awareness required to play it successfully. In order to evade all the incoming spherical missiles, you have to be constantly aware of your opponents in front of you, as well as those "in prison" behind you.

To be an exceptional dodgeball player, you need an extra set of eyes in the back of your head. Powers of 360-degree observation are an immense aid in detecting well-placed sorties. I still remember the stock crucial warning shouted out by teammates on the sidelines: "Heads up!" which meant "Watch out for incoming enemy fire!"

In Proverbs 22:3, and again in Proverbs 27:12, the wisdom of the ages calls loudly, "Heads up!" "The prudent sees the evil and hides himself, but the naïve go on, and are punished for it." In other words, the prudent are well aware of what is going on all around them, so they are able to heed the warning and step out of harm's way. The wise are not ignorant of the dangers and the inevitable consequences those dangers pose. The naïve, on the other hand, succumb to the seductive riptides of present danger and are imperceptibly drawn further out to open sea.

When it comes to the issues discussed in this book, the church can ill-afford to ignore the gay-rights agenda with all of its various tentacles. To that end, I have been archiving articles for several years related to this movement and its surrogates. What follows is a small sample that illustrates the moral threat the movement presents to the church and society at large. The following headlines serve to buttress the points already made in this book. The primary motivation for including this information is simply to yell, "Heads up!" one more time before you place the book back on the shelf.

California screaming

The event garnering the lion's share of headlines at the time of writing is the ban on gay marriage passed by California state voters in the recent elections (November 4, 2008).[1]

On May 15, 2008, the California State Supreme Court overturned a previous ban on gay marriage that defined marriage as an exclusive union between a man and a woman. In the 2000 election, California voters had passed Proposition 22, effectively banning SSM in the golden state. Proposition 22 passed easily by a margin of 61 per cent to 39 per cent. There were numerous attempts by Democratic state legislators to circumvent the will of the people, but in the end it was judicial activism that overturned the sentiment of the overwhelming majority. Once the liberal court torpedoed Proposition 22, the floodgates were open for 18,000 gay couples to marry officially.

Conservatives responded to the court's decision by sponsoring another ballot initiative, Proposition 8, which would go further than the previous initiative, calling for an amendment to the state constitution defining marriage as an exclusive union between a man and a woman. This referendum by the people and for the people passed 52 per cent to 48 per cent. The hotly contested ballot cost Californians the princely sum of $74 million, making Proposition 8 the costliest ballot initiative in the USA. Against all realistic odds—the media, Hollywood, San Francisco politics, generous contributors like Apple, Google, and Yahoo—the initiative passed by 4 per cent!

This brought the immediate and obligatory protest reaction from gay-rights activists all over California. These protests subsequently spilled over into other major cities across the USA. In one protest near Palm Springs, California, a sixty-nine-year-old lady was trampled and the Styrofoam cross she was carrying to protest against the protesters was trampled upon.[2] There were also reports of bystanders hurling eggs and insults at protestors. The mood and response to Proposition 8 has been quite ugly.

Amid the cacophony of bombast, Scott Eckern, the director of the Sacramento theater, was forced to resign his post because he donated $1,000 for Proposition 8.[3] Eckern lamented, "I am disappointed that my personal convictions have cost me the opportunity to do what I love the most." So much for the tolerance and compassion often called for by those promoting the gay agenda. Blacklisting and bullying tactics are favorites in the gay-rights arsenal.

Needless to say, the protest against Proposition 8 has not left the church unscathed. At a gathering in Roanoke, Virginia, Tony Campolo, no stranger to controversy, railed against Proposition 8 and those who voted for it.4 Though Campolo claims to be conservative on the issue of homosexuality, he nonetheless asked, "What did we win? ... I'll tell you what we won. We won tens of thousands of gays and lesbians parading up and down the streets ... screaming against the church, seeing the church as enemy." He continued, "I don't know how we're going to reach these brothers and sisters."

What Campolo needs to consider is that you never reach anyone for Christ when you approve of their sin. Though we must respond redemptively to the homosexual community, we cannot gloss over their sin. The truth must accompany the love. The tension of the two is needed in the outreach enterprise.

My question for Campolo is, did Christ ever approve of and overlook the sin of those whom he sought to reach? Did he approve of and overlook the Samaritan woman's sin of rampant immorality in John 4? Did Christ approve of the rich young ruler's sin of greed and covetousness? No, and as a result, the rich young ruler went away sorrowful. Did Christ approve of and overlook the sin in the woman caught in adultery in John 8? No, he said, "Go, and sin no more." Did Paul approve of and overlook the sin of idolatry in Ephesus in Acts 19? Hardly—and a melee ensued. As evangelist Ray Comfort, from the Way of The Master, is fond of reminding us, the gospel message always includes "Law to the proud, and grace to the humble."

Perhaps Campolo has forgotten that "Righteousness exalts a nation, but sin is a disgrace to any people" (Prov. 14:34). Therefore, Proposition 8 was and is the right way to go, irrespective of the consequences and actions of its opponents. The biblical principles for marriage and family are the backbone of any nation, and, once jettisoned, societal decay and degeneration are accelerated.

To date, Proposition 8 has elicited three separate law suits. The main argument behind the law suits is that SSM is a civil-rights issue, and therefore voters do not have the authority to decide on it. So once again, the California State Supreme Court will hear the arguments and render a decision.

What is evident in this instance is that the will of the people through the democratic process is irrelevant and of no consequence to gay-rights activists and their supporters, such as Democrat Senators Feinstein and Boxer, as well as Governor Schwarzenegger.

From my very limited knowledge, I cannot predict the eventual outcome, but leaving this issue to a very liberal court does not bode well for the promoters of Proposition 8. But God is always able!

Without a US Constitutional Marriage Amendment Act defining marriage, the SSM lobby will continue to gain ground one state at a time, using liberal courts and *ad hominem* promotions to gain public support. Given that the Democratic Party now occupies the White House, the Senate, and Congress, it seems quite unlikely that there is going to be a US constitutional amendment defining marriage any time soon.

Gay pride goes to church

Beyond the Proposition 8 flap, there is a tremendous amount of activity on the gay-rights front around the world. Much of it is aimed at the church. Some comes from inside the professing church itself.

In November 2007, Anglican Archbishop Desmond Tutu went on a verbal rampage defending homosexuality in his denomination.[5] His diatribe was primarily directed at the ongoing mess over priest Gene Robinson, who is openly gay. Robinson was appointed Bishop over New Hampshire in the USA. As a result of this appointment, many have either left the denomination or are threatening to leave.

Tutu emotionally stated that the Anglican Church appeared "extraordinarily homophobic" because of opposition to Robinson's promotion. Continuing his rant, he said, "If God as they say is homophobic I wouldn't worship that God."

Because Tutu is an icon in South Africa, coverage of his outburst dominated the headlines there. In response, I wrote the following rebuttal, which appeared in a few of the local papers:

Dear Editor,

In his latest diatribe ("I wouldn't worship an anti-gay God") Desmond Tutu gave a clinic on the use of *ad hominem* logic. Tutu's hurling of acerbic invective at his detractors is a favorite smokescreen to cloud the weakness of his own arguments on homosexuality and same-sex marriage.

Tutu's transvalued (calling good evil and evil good) viewpoint on this issue has far more in common with a postmodern, pluralistic culture than the Bible. For Tutu to argue as he does, he must supplant the Bible with the popular interposing of a politically correct culture. To achieve this, he, like many today, must ignore the obvious and argue the ridiculous. This he has done well!

The question arising from Tutu's tantrum is whether or not God is "anti-gay." Rather, the question should be, is God anti-sin (adultery, fornication, lying, theft, corruption, pride, homosexuality, etc.)? The answer is an unequivocal "yes."

Because God is a complex of attributes, including infinite holiness, righteousness, and justice—not just love—he will not "welcome" any sin into his presence. This is precisely why God sent his only begotten Son to die and serve as the perfect sacrifice for humanity's sin. For those who repent from their sin on the basis of Christ's finished work on the cross, there is forgiveness and the eternal embrace of a welcoming God! But God only welcomes those who come on his terms.

Therefore, the real question isn't "Is God anti-gay?", but "Is Tutu pro-God?"
Revd Mark Christopher
Living Hope Bible Church

More recently, the Moreleta Park NG Kerk (Dutch Reformed Church) in Pretoria, South Africa lost a court case initiated by a gay employee who was fired when it was discovered he was a practicing homosexual.[6] When approached about the sin, the man had refused to repent, so the church, in accordance with its policy, had terminated his musical services.

As part of the settlement, the church was ordered to pay the plaintiff 87,000 rand (12,000 US dollars at that time) and to apologize unconditionally to the plaintiff, with all of which the church complied.

This was seen as a landmark case for the church in South Africa. Many people, myself included, urged the church to appeal against the judgment to the constitutional court level, which Moreleta Park ultimately chose not to do. The moral of the story for the rest of us is to have a well-defined employment policy in place carefully outlining what is and is not acceptable and detailing disciplinary procedures should an employee be found in breach of the stated policy.

In the US state of Michigan on Sunday, November 9, 2008, a radical gay-rights group called Bash Back disrupted the morning services at Mount Hope Church.[7] As the pastor got up to pray, protestors, already in the pews, jumped up and began running up and down aisles throwing pamphlets and condoms at congregants while yelling "It's OK to be gay" and "Jesus was a homo."

Protestors then pulled a fire alarm and unfurled a banner from the balcony. Simultaneously, outside the church, protestors carried signs with an upside-down pink cross. In an interview with a church official aired on FOX News, the church was seen to be very measured and gracious in its response. Mount Hope demonstrated a far greater degree of respect and tolerance than was accorded them.

Given the recent political victory for gay-rights activists in an Obama presidency combined with their levels of desperation to see comprehensive gay-rights legislation, it should not surprise the American church to see an increase in these kinds of incidents in the near future.

Staying in the state of Michigan, Bradley LaShawn Fowler, who is gay, was reported in July 2008 to be suing Christian publishing giants Zondervan and Thomas Nelson for violating his constitutional rights by misinterpreting the Bible.[8] Fowler claimed that certain versions of the Bible mistranslate words in the original language into the English word "homosexual," maintaining that this is a deliberate change, not an accurate translation. As a result, Fowler said, this term "homosexual" produces irreparable harm to the gay community, so he was suing Zondervan for $60 million and Thomas Nelson for $10 million.

I have confidence that the attorneys for both Zondervan and Thomas Nelson will point out to the court that biblical words translated "drunkards," "adulterer," "fornicator," "thief," "liar," and "murderer" could make any number of people suffer mental and emotional distress. Just think of the litigation that could be generated by participants in any of those sins!

South of Michigan, from Cedarville University in the state of Ohio comes an astonishing article from the student newspaper, *Cedars*.[9] It was written by a student promoting SSM. The reason why this is considered news is because Cedarville has a long tradition of being a bastion for conservative, Bible-believing teaching. When I was applying to Christian colleges twenty-five years ago, Cedarville was one of the schools I seriously considered.

In the article, the student journalist interviews Nikki, supposedly a Christian homosexual. In the middle of this pretentious treatise on SSM, the writer blurts out, "I am still vexed by arguments against the legalizing of gay marriage." In the conclusion, Nikki unconvincingly argues that "Every person should be able to find happiness. You may not understand me, and I may not understand you, but we should nonetheless love and accept one another."

In this, Nikki egregiously makes happiness the sum of life and living. But for the Christian, the primary pursuit of life is holiness in Christ: "but like the Holy One who called you, be holy yourselves also in all your behavior; because it is written, 'You shall be holy, for I am holy'" (1 Peter 1:15–16). It is only when the Christian strives for Christlike holiness, by God's enabling grace, that true happiness is found. The pursuit of happiness devoid of holiness has selfishness as its sum.

Loving and respecting those with whom we disagree is essential, but this does not include acceptance and approval of their flagrant violations of God's Word. If Nikki truly loves her neighbor as herself, she will not coerce others' opinions through the present-day lines of gay-rights manipulation.

Though I do not believe the faculty and board of Cedarville endorse the article, the fact that it was printed is a troubling sign and signals just how pervasive gay-rights activism has become. When the citadels of conservative theological thought and belief begin flirting with the pernicious promotions of SSM, someone needs to yell "Heads up!"

In news that has just broken as I write, Christian internet-dating site eHarmony has been sued by Eric McKinley, a gay man, for discriminating against gays.[10] McKinley maintained that eHarmony had not been catering to the homosexual community. Those running eHarmony were persuaded by their attorneys to settle rather than wait for a probable negative verdict. Given that there are hundreds of dating sites that cater exclusively to gays, it was not as if McKinley was being deprived of an opportunity to hook up online. This is another instance of using the courts to legislate acceptance of the gay lifestyle.

In her editorial on this case, Michelle Malkin of Investor's Business Daily noted, "This case is akin to a meat-eater suing a vegetarian restaurant for not offering him a rib-eye ..." In the end, eHarmony capitulated to the bullying offensive of McKinley. Malkin lamented that "capitulation will only yield a worse, entirely predictable outcome: more shakedowns of private businesses that hold views deemed unacceptable by the Equality-at-All-Costs-Brigade."

For those who still cling to the misguided assumption that the gay community is just going to peacefully coexist with the church once it is granted comprehensive gay-rights legislation, consider an academic journal article I came across in my research: "Conservative Christian Teachers: Possible Consequences for Lesbian, Gay and Bisexual Youth."[11]

The gist of the article tries to tag Bible-believing Christianity as the primary culprit for the stigma and negative stereotypes associated with being LBGT. The remedy, according to the writer, is to force those who disagree with homosexuality to play ball:

Individuals who cling to homophobic beliefs *must* want to look at different perspectives. Individuals who feel that LGB issues have nothing to do with them *must* feel connected. Those who believe that sexual identity is only part of the home and not of the community, which in large part has decided what sexual identity [it] is appropriate to have, *must redefine family* and community values. Students need to *explore their own subjectivity* and to understand that they are *active agents* in how they *construct themselves and others*. Future educators who refuse to take these steps can cause irreparable damage [emphasis added].

It is quite explicit. Those who see LGBT behavior as wrong "must" be made to see their error and acknowledge it. Since most pattern their views and values on what is learned in the home, then the home or family "must" be redefined along with various "community" values, like those learned in church. Then students, rather than listening to those external rules from home and church, need to take a long journey through the inner spaces of their own subjective selves to arrive at a more equitable value system, which is self-constructed. The message is unmistakable: "Don't believe what you were taught in those traditionally homophobic institutions. Instead, go your own way; 'follow your heart' is the general rule of thumb, but just make sure you believe what we want you to believe!" So much for encouraging students to think independently.

While promoters of this brand of logic are having a measure of success with this tactic in the Christian-influenced West, I wonder how this kind of coercion would work in Islamic countries?

All this illustrates that, at least in the West, there is a concerted and well-orchestrated effort to both demonize and criminalize Christian opposition to homosexuality. But the church must not lose its way. We must recognize and confront the dangers while simultaneously responding redemptively to those who wish to oppress us with their agenda. "Heads up!"

Transcending gender all the way to the maternity ward

Part and parcel of the SSM agenda is to promote the whole notion of transgenderism, which includes transvestites who cross-dress and transsexuals who opt for gender-reassignment surgery. For their part, the media endeavor to portray this as perfectly normal and acceptable. The roots of transgender thinking are anchored in the soil of the belief that all humans are a complex of both male and female. Based on this, its proponents say, it is perfectly normal to explore the other side of one's gender makeup. Yet the Bible is unambiguous on this point, for God made them "male and female." Even nature testifies to this. When was the last time you saw a cross-dressing bear or a transgender lion?

There have been many examples of the transgender agenda in the headlines that should be cause for concern. The 2008 elections in the USA produced the first openly transgendered mayor in America's history.[12] In Silverton, Oregon, Stu Rasmussen, a transvestite, became mayor with distinction: Mayor Rasmussen is a cross-dresser. Rasmussen has been described as a "dude" with a distinctly "masculine voice" but having the fashion sense of "Alaska Governor Sarah Palin." Rasmussen describes himself as "… a heterosexual male who appears to be a female." What is so tragic is that many believe that having a mayor who wears eye shadow, a skirt, and pumps, all with a five o'clock shadow, is progress. No doubt this is progress, but it is progress in the wrong direction.

Another eye-catching headline, this time from Australia, reads "Little Maxine Wants to Be Max." The story relates how a twelve-year-old girl wants to undergo gender-reassignment surgery to become a boy.[13] The girl's estranged father opposed these efforts, and a multiphase court case ensued. Up to the time of writing, the judge has been sympathetic to the girl's plight by approving hormone implants to stop menstruation and prevent the growth of breasts and hips. Surgery will have to wait until the girl is eighteen years of age. All of this treatment, I assume, will be compliments of the Australian taxpayer?

Then there is the ever-popular Thomas Beatie, who has been hailed as the world's first pregnant male. Beatie, openly transsexual, is, at the time of writing, now pregnant with her second child. During the first pregnancy, Beatie said, "How does it feel to be a pregnant man? Incredible."[14]

The media do not even try to challenge this erroneous thinking that Beatie is a man. Most in the media seem ostensibly to think that gender is a socially constructed concept that can be reoriented given enough exposure and media coverage. But the biological reality is that, contrary to her male-like appearance, Beatie is a surgically modified female. No amount of headlining or shock-jock reporting to the contrary will ever alter the realities of biology.

Rock-a-bye-baby: robbing the cradle

A recent headline in South Africa announced, "Teacher Wants to Marry 12-yr-old Sweetheart."[15] The girl, who was thirteen at the time of the report, miscarried her second child by her high-school teacher, who was twenty-three. Understandably, the education department was investigating this situation. For her part, the mother of the girl said, "I will not separate my child from the man she loves because they go way back. He paid compensation for the first child and is at present paying Lobola [a dowry]."

The question must be asked, what does a thirteen-year-old girl know about love and all its attendant responsibilities? If the girl was only thirteen, how far back could her relationship with her teacher have gone?

The girl's mother rationalized the acceptability of this moral outrage on the basis of monetary compensation, as if morality were on the fiscal auction block.

Another incident concerning the exploitation of a twelve-year-old girl found a Muslim cleric in Indonesia being probed by Indonesian police.[16] The cleric was also planning to wed other girls who were aged only seven and nine. The forty-three-year-old man defended his marriage to the twelve-year-old by saying she had already reached puberty. According to some Islamic scholars, such pedogomic (intergenerational) marriages are permissible under Islamic law.

Concerning pedogamy, there is already a concerted effort on the part of some liberally minded activists to get the United Nations and liberally minded countries to change and lower their age-of-consent laws. Is this really so far-fetched? Consider that, in many countries, a twelve-year-old girl can get an abortion without parental consent (see Chapter 3 under "Pedogamy"). Allowing twelve-year-old girls access to birth control and abortion without parental consent already implies that the age of sexual consent is twelve years of age.

But how will this ever be justified? By using children's rights arguments and the amoral logic of "If they really love each other and mutually consent, whose business is it?", liberal lawmakers will gradually move further in this direction in the years to come. What is to stop them? Valueless values?

Sexual freedom-fighters and the fruits of free love

As I asked earlier in the book, how did we get to today's sexually permissive and promiscuous point? How has the unthinkable become thinkable? Undeniably, we live in an age that is almost completely bereft of sexual morals and ethics. The process of transvaluing sexuality has produced an almost wholesale abandonment of any biblically derived standards for all things sexual.

In answer to the question: the sexual revolution, which began in earnest in the 1960s, has blossomed and now produced the fruit of free love. Yet sexual Xanadu remains elusive. What many never realized was that the sexual revolution was and is a package deal to include homosexuality.

Premarital relationships and live-in situations helped pave the way for today's omnisexual, pansexual super-highway. Once fornication and living together were tolerated and accepted, the focus shifted to homosexuality. Once homosexuality is accepted, you can expect the focus to shift to other deviancies on the sexual horizon. This will not stop until there is nothing left to the imagination.

The following headlines illustrate that the sexual revolution is not dead but has metastasized to its present cultural malignancy by promoting an anything-goes approach.

As I pound out these words at my keyboard, almost every radio station around the world is airing the current hit song by Kate Perry, "I Kissed a Girl." The line adds, "and I liked it." Seven-year-olds are walking down the street tethered to iPods and bopping to this snappy little sonnet, "I kissed a girl and I liked it." Slowly and subtly, this verbal assault is eroding the defenses of many an adolescent.

FOX News sexpert, Yvonne Fulbright, wryly admitted the strength of the song's lyric, confessing, "Actually, I've never kissed a girl. And I haven't the foggiest clue if I'd actually like it. But the playfully seductive words from Kate Perry's 'I Kissed a Girl' certainly got me thinking: Would I? Could I?"[17]

While one song will not break the moral bank, Hollywood, combined with all its willing accomplices, has been incrementally eroding our sense of right and wrong one song and one movie at a time.

One of the more disturbing headlines was from the LA Times: "Bestiality Doc Premiers at Sundance."[18] The journalist reviews a documentary on bestiality which debuted at Robert Redford's Sundance Film Festival in 2007. The director of the documentary described his movie, entitled *Zoo*, as dealing with "the last taboo, the boundary of something comprehensible." Sadly, he has more insight than most. Once bestiality becomes permissible, there is nowhere else to go, as you have reached the bottom of the moral basement. But Robert Redford does not care.

Just as disturbing as *Zoo* is a Broadway musical entitled *Spring Awakening*. This hit musical details the teenage angst and frustration of high-school students and their subsequent "sexual awakening in repressed 19th-century Germany."[19] One reviewer enthused that *Spring Awakening* is "a straight shot of eroticism" as it "tastefully" broaches controversial issues like abortion, homosexuality, sadomasochism, and abuse. If one considers nude teenagers performing various sex acts on stage "tasteful," then *Spring Awakening* fits the bill.

Another gay-rights incident occurred just prior to the 2008 US elections. A kindergarten teacher in Hayward, California coaxed her four- and five-year-old students to sign a pledge card supporting homosexuals and homosexual rights.[20]

According to press reports, the cards asked the very impressionable youngsters to be "an ally" and to pledge not to use LGBT—lesbian, gay, bisexual, transgender—language or slurs. Further, the children were asked to "intervene, when I feel I can, in situations where others are using anti-LGBT language …"

Who can deny that such tactics amount to brainwashing and crass indoctrination? Tremendous pressure is being forced upon the innocence of youth to accept the philosophy of pro-homosexual attitudes and agendas. My question is, how many four- and five-year-olds know what a lesbian, gay, bisexual, or transgendered person is? How does one even begin to explain such complex concepts to those so young?

This very disturbing incident signals that in many schools around the world, education is a thing of the past, being replaced by the social engineering of the politically correct jet set. It is no wonder Jonny can matriculate, but struggles to read and is ignorant of the most basic general knowledge.

Just when you think it can't get any worse, the UK *Times Online* appears with this provocative headline: "I Had Sex with my Brother but I Don't Feel Guilty."[21] The trailer beneath the title explains, "A woman slept with her sibling for years and has good memories. Not many people understand their relationship, she says." It was obvious from the comments section from online readers that most approved and applauded such "honesty" and "openness." I wonder how "open" and "tolerant" these same incest enthusiasts would be if it were their own children? The absence of guilt in such matters is evidence that society has a seared conscience.

In the latest scientific advance, LiveScience.Com asked "Are Humans Meant To Be Monogamous?"[22] Some so-called experts, basing their work on evolutionary theory, have concluded that humans are meant to be "mildly polygynous," which means that a male is meant to mate with more than one female. Just the justification many a libido-laden man wants to hear. The researchers in this study distinguish between being "sexually monogamous" and "socially monogamous." "Sexual monogamy" means one sexual partner for life, while "social monogamy" refers to someone who cheats on his wife, but stays with the family.

In a book released in 2008, sexologist Dr. Baruch Banai claims that humans are still far too sexually repressed.[23] The central thesis in *Sex: The Fundamental Attraction* outlines the steps needed to help society walk through the threshold to "sexual freedom." Dr. Banai maintains that when it comes to sex, "nobody talks about it." I am not sure what world Dr. Banai lives in, because in my world, a person has extreme difficulty avoiding talk about sex. Everywhere we turn, we are confronted with salacious ads, sexually charged songs, seductive magazines, the temptation of the Internet, x-rated discussions around the water-cooler at work, and television; all do their bit to convince us that it is OK to do whatever we want to do, as long as we don't hurt anyone. There are even political parties, such as the new Australian Sex Party, devoted to the cause of pushing the moral boundaries beyond belief.

The wizards of the sexual revolution are perplexed and downright confused by all the headlines that showcase the ill-effects of their message of sexual emancipation. Here are a few "Heads up!" articles that indicate all is not well with the sexual revolution:

- Consequences: "In 10 Months 1000 Girls Pregnant: Report."[24] In the South African province (state) of Mpumalanga, 1,000 school-age girls became pregnant in a ten-month period in 2007. One school in the Tembisa township area had 100 pregnant girls alone. Obviously the message of "safe sex" has not gotten through, or maybe it has in an unintended way. The Education Department will no doubt respond with more sex education.
- Consequences: "Our Children are Raping Each Other."[25] Imagine a five-year-old boy assaulting a three-year-old girl. Children in South Africa—as well as in most other parts of the world—are becoming

more sexually aggressive and are going to court for indecent assault. But the authorities have yet to connect the dots. Tragic, but true.

- Consequences: "Rise in Child Sex Crimes."[26] South African officials say they are aware of this problem, but seem clueless on how society got here and what to do about it.

- Consequences: "Meet Cape's Sex-Crazed Children."[27] This article details how primary-school-age boys (five to twelve years old), predominately in the gang-infested Cape Flats, are sodomizing one another in school restrooms and worse. One school principal claims that the source of the problem is in the socio-economic conditions. While I am sure such unfortunate conditions do not help the problem, it is really a moral crisis that finds its roots in the breakdown of the traditional family, which is the active ingredient in a healthy society.

- Consequences: "Is Sex Education Failing Young People?"[28] After asking this question, education experts proceed to prescribe an even more comprehensive sex-education program. This is what happens when parents abdicate their duties to the school system. Forty-plus years of state-sponsored sex education has only made things worse, not better. Allowing the world to "educate" in this area is much like having a blind person serve as a guide in the Louvre.

- Consequences: In the UK, Explorer Scouts are now going to take scout field trips to local health clinics to be better educated on sex and the use of condoms.[29] This is nothing less then a rank admission that sex education in UK schools has been an abysmal failure.

Such an avalanche of secular folly is best described by Solomon, who said, "Fools mock at sin, but among the upright there is good will" (Prov. 14:9). This proverb highlights the callous unconcern fools have for all the mayhem they generate because of their ungodly views and actions. Ironically, what they do is often done out of professed compassion and concern for others. Yet they fail to see the extreme damage they cause. In contrast, the upright preserve goodwill toward God and others with both their doctrines and their deeds!

In moral insolence, the promoters of the free-love creed evidence a seeming unconcern about the damage they have produced. When the folly of their ways and the failure of their prescriptions are pointed out, they scornfully respond in scoffing and militant tones. But the upright of God say what they say not because they lack compassion; on the contrary, it is because we desire to advance God's general goodwill for all. God's Word has the answers for the sexual web of deceit spun by the sexual revolution, and we are the channels for communicating the very breath of God on the matter.

The church of Christ must not grow weary in the well-doing of advancing God's will in this area. Recognizing the evil should drive us to prayer, promote the study of God's Word related to the issue, encourage the guarding of our own hearts, and provoke the instruction of our children in both word and deed. We must strive to live with the tension of confronting the sin while responding redemptively, and we must speak up as the world seeks to drown our voices. May every shepherd warn his flock by cupping his hands and shouting "Heads up!" For the King is coming!

Notes

1 "Voters Approve Proposition 8 Banning Same-Sex Marriages," November 5, 2008, latimes.com/news/local/la-me-gaymarriage5-2008nov05,0,1545381.story.

2 "Cross-Bearing Woman Says She was Attacked by Gay Marriage Supporters, May Press Charges," November 13, 2008, foxnews.com/story/0,2933,450884,00.html.

3 "Sacramento Theater Director Resigns in Prop. 8 Aftermath," November 13, 2008, latimes.com/entertainment/la-et-quick13-2008nov13,0,7115878.story.

4 "BGAV Reduces Budget; Tony Campolo Tells Messengers He Opposed Calif. Prop. 8," November 18, 2008, bpnews.net/bpnews.asp?ID=29361.

5 "Tutu Blasts Church for Gay 'Obsession,'" November 18, 2007, iol.co.za/index.php?set_id=1&click_id=13&art_id=nw20071118082911437C558373.

6 "Church Says Sorry to Gay Teacher," September 11, 2009, iol.co.za/index.php?set_id=1&click_id=13&art_id=nw20080911135051162C194817.

7 "Gay Rights Protestors Disrupt Sunday Service," accessed November 12, 2008, lansingstatejournal.com/article/20081112/NEWS01/811120369.

8 "Bible Publishers Sued for Anti-Gay References," July 10, 2008, newsmax.com/insidecover/man_sues_bible_publishers/2008/07/10/111626.html.

9 "More Intriguing Views from Cedarville University: Student Newspaper Calls for Christians to Support Gay Marriage," accessed April 12, 2008, theworldfrommywindow.blogspot.com/2007/06/more-intriguing-views-from-cedarville.html.

10 "The Coercion Of Tolerance At eHarmony," November 21, 2008, ibdeditorials.com/IBDArticles.aspx?id=312155794628865&kw=EHarmony.

11 Michele Malamud Kahn, "Conservative Christian Teachers: Possible Consequences for Lesbian, Gay and Bisexual Youth," *Intercultural Education*, 17:4 (2006), p. 366.

12 "Oregon Town Elects Nation's First Transgender Mayor," November 8, 2008, komonews.com/news/local/34147009.html.

13 "Court Clears 12-yr-old to Undergo Sex Change," May 25, 2008, timesofindia.indiatimes.com/World/Its_a_Mad_Mad_World/Court_clears_12-yr-old_to_undergo_sex_change/articleshow/3070834.cms.

14 See "'Pregnant Man' Gives Birth—Reports," July 4, 2008, iol.co.za/index.php?set_id=1&click_id=31&art_id=nw20080704110740744C483135,. Also "Oregon Woman Who Said She Had Sex Change Now Claims 'He's' Pregnant," March 26, 2008, foxnews.com/story/0,2933,341595,00.html.

15 "Teacher Wants to Marry 12-yr-old Sweetheart," September 26, 2008, iol.co.za/index.php?set_id=1&click_id=13&art_id=vn20080926112334137C168576.

16 "Cops Probe Cleric who Married 12-year-old," October 28, 2008, iol.co.za/index.php?set_id=1&click_id=3&art_id=nw20081028120646700C628407.

17 "FOXSexpert: I Kissed a Girl and I liked It—Embracing Your Sexual Fluidity," November 17 2008, foxnews.com/story/0,2933,453527,00.html.

18 "'Zoo': The Skillfully Made Documentary Examines Bestiality as a Lifestyle," May 4, 2007, theenvelope.latimes.com/cl-et-zoo4may04,0,3150844.story.

19 "Erotic New Musical a Surprise Hit on Broadway," January 21, 2007, reuters.com/article/artsNews/idUSN1934645120070122.

20 "School Clams Up on 'Gay' Pledge Cards Given to Kindergartners," November 1, 2008, foxnews.com/story/0,2933,445865,00.html.

21 "I Had Sex with my Brother but I Don't Feel Guilty," July 15, 2008, women.timesonline.co.uk/tol/life_and_style/women/families/article4332635.ece.

22 "Are Humans Meant To Be Monogamous?", accessed November 8, 2008, livescience.com/mysteries/080319-llm-monogamy.html.

23 "We're Not Close to Sex Freedom," November 3, 2008, iol.co.za/index.php?set_id=1&click_id=13&art_id=vn20081103052506172C962283.

24 "In 10 Months 1000 Girls Pregnant: Report," December 4, 2007, iol.co.za/index.php?set_id=1&click_id=13&art_id=nw20071204074948503C256178.

25 "Our Children are Raping Each Other," November 18, 2007, thetimes.co.za/PrintEdition/Article.aspx?id=616379.

26 "Rise in Child Sex Crimes," *The Star*, March 27, 2007, p. 1.

27 "Meet Cape's 'Sex-Crazed' Children," *The Cape Argus*, September 19, 2008, p. 3.

28 "Is Sex Education Failing Young People?", August 6, 2008, iolhivaids.co.za/index.php?fSectionId=1591&fArticleId=4545725.

29 "'We Should Be Realistic about Teenagers and Sex,'" October 21, 2008, iolhivaids.co.za/index.php?fSectionId=1591&fArticleId=4671806.

Note: The works marked with an asterisk (*) are those I highly recommend.

AFP-SAPA, "No Sex Please, We're Canadians: Sex Party Hard Put to Get Rise out of Voters," *The Cape Times*, May 18, 2005, p. 4.

Anon, "Dad's Love is Different from Mom's Love," accessed March 19, 2007, iol.co.za/htm/frame_babynet.php?click_id=694.

Anon, "Homosexual Unions: Rare and Fragile," April 17, 2007, at worldcongress.org.

Bailey, Michael J, Dunne, Michael P., and **Martin, Nicolas G.,** "Genetic and Environmental Influences on Sexual Orientation and its Correlates in an Australian Twin Sample," *Journal of Personality and Social Psychology*, 78 (March 2000).

Balch, David L., (ed.), *Homosexuality, Science, and the "Plain Sense" of Scripture* (Grand Rapids, MI: Eerdmans, 2000).

Beck, James R., "Evangelicals, Homosexuality, and Social Science," *Journal of Evangelical Theological Society*, 40:1 (1997), pp. 83–97.

Belz, Joel, "A Totally Alien Mindset: Homosexuals and Others are Demanding Approval, Not just Permission, for their Behavior," March 20, 2004, at worldmag.com.

Botha, Peet, *The Bible and Homosex: Sexual Truths for a Modern Society* (Kranskop, South Africa: Khanya Press, 2005).*

Brown, Paul E., (ed.), *Homosexuality: Christian Truth and Love* (Leominster: Day One, 2007).*

Bruce, Tammy, *The Death of Right and Wrong* (New York: Three Rivers, 2003).*

Busenitz, Irvin A., "Marriage and Homosexuality: Toward a Biblical Understanding," *The Master's Seminary Journal* 19:2 (2008), pp. 203–216.*

Carbone, June, "Morality, Public Policy and the Family: The Role of Marriage and the Public–Private Divide", accessed November 5, 2008, at scu.edu.

Clark, Kathleen M., et. al, "A Longitudinal Study of Religiosity and Mortality Risk," *Journal of Health Psychology*, 4:3 (1999), pp. 381–391.

Cole, Sherwood O., "Biology, Homosexuality, and Moral Culpability," *Bibliotheca Sacra*, 154:615 (1997), pp. 355–366.

Daily, Timothy J., Ph.D., "Comparing the Lifestyle of Homosexual Couples to Married Couples," accessed August 9, 2007, at frc.org.

De Young, James B., *Homosexuality: Contemporary Claims Examined in Light of the Bible and Other Ancient Literature and Law* (Grand Rapids, MI: Kregel, 2001).*

Diggs, John Jr., MD, "The Health Risks of Gay Sex," 2002, at corporateresourcecouncil.org.*

The Editors, "Nuclear Fission," August 9, 2003, at worldmag.com.

Select bibliography

Ellison, Marvin M., *Same-Sex Marriage? A Christian Analysis* (Cleveland, OH: Pilgrim, 2004).

Evangelical Alliance Policy Commission, *Transsexuality: A Report by the Evangelical Alliance Commission* (London, UK: Evangelical Alliance, 2000).

Evans, Jenni, "Constitutional Court Battle over Gay Marriage Begins," *The Cape Times*, May 18, 2005.

Foust, Michael, "Mass. 'Gay Marriage'" Numbers Plummet," May 25, 2007, at bpnews.net.

Gagnon, Robert A. J., "Barack Obama's Disturbing Misreading of the Sermon on the Mount as Support for Homosexual Sex," October 23, 2008, at robgagnon.net.*

——"Obama's Coming War on Historic Christianity over Homosexual Practice and Abortion," November 2, 2008, at robgagnon.net.*

——*The Bible and Homosexual Practice: Texts and Hermeneutics* (Nashville, TN: Abingdon Press, 2001).*

Gelman, David, et al, "Born or Bred?" *Newsweek*, February 24, 1992, p. 48.

Grenz, Stanley J., *A Primer on Postmodernism* (Grand Rapids, MI: Eerdmans, 1996).

Grisanti, Michael A., "Cultural and Medical Myths about Homosexuality," *The Master's Seminary Journal*, 19:2 (2008), pp. 175–202.*

Gudal, Joseph P., "Homosexuality: Fact and Fiction," accessed August 17, 2004, at equip.org.

——"That which is Unnatural: Homosexuality in Society, the Church, and Scripture," accessed August 17, 2004, at equip.org.

Heimbach, Daniel, *True Sexual Morality: Recovering Biblical Standards for a Culture in Crisis* Wheaton, IL: Crossway, 2004).*

Holland, Richard L., "Christian Parenting and Homosexuality," *The Master's Seminary Journal*, 19:2 (2008), pp. 217–231.*

[Independent] "Sperm Donor Must Pay Child Support," October 14, 2005, at iol.co.za.

Irvine, Martha, "Bois and Grrls Come out to Play as Youth Bend Gender," *The Cape Times*, March 11, 2005.

Jenson, Phillip D., and **Tony Payne,** *Pure Sex* (Kingsford, NSW: Matthias Media, 1998).

Jones, Peter, "Are We Goin' to San Francisco?", August 7, 2007, at truthxchange.com.

——*The God of Sex: How Spirituality Defines Your Sexuality* (Colorado Springs, CO: Victor, 2006).*

——*Pagans in the Pews* (Ventura, CA: Regal, 2001).*

Jones, Stanton L., and **Yarhouse, Mark A.,** *Homosexuality: The Use of Scientific Research in the Church's Moral Debate* (Downers Grove, IL: IVP, 2000).*

Kahn, Michele Malamud, "Conservative Christian Teachers: Possible Consequences for Lesbian, Gay and Bisexual Youth," *Intercultural Education*, 17:4 (2006), pp. 359–371.

Kennedy, D. James, and **Newcombe, Jerry,** *What's Wrong with Same-Sex Marriage?* (Wheaton, IL: Crossway, 2004).*

Kinsley, Michael, "Abolish Marriage: Let's Really Get the Government out of our Bedrooms," *Washington Post*, July 3, 2003, A23.

Koop, C. Everett, and **Schaeffer, Francis,** *Whatever Happened to the Human Race?* (Wheaton, IL: Crossway, 1983).

Kostenberger, Andreas J., and **Jones, David W.,** *God, Marriage, and Family: Rebuilding the Biblical Foundation* (Wheaton, IL: Crossway, 2004).*

Lofton, John, "Rape and Evolution: Evolution Shows its True Colours," *Creation Magazine*, 23:4 (2001), pp. 50–53.

Lutzer, Erwin W., *The Truth about Same-Sex Marriage: 6 Things You Need to Know about What's Really at Stake* (Chicago: Moody Press, 2004).*

MacArthur, John, "God's Word on Homosexuality: The Truth about Sin and the Reality of Forgiveness," *The Master's Seminary Journal*, 19:2 (2008), pp. 153–174.*

Maier, Bill, and **Stanton, Glenn T.,** *Marriage on Trial: The Case against Same-Sex Marriage and Parenting* (Downers Grove: IVP, 2004).*

McKie, Robin, and **McVeigh, Tracy,** "Scientists' Claim that Rape is about Sex not Violence Outrages Feminists," January 16, 2000, at guardian.co.uk.

Mohler, Albert, Jr., "The Case against Homosexual Marriage," January 15, 2004, at crosswalk.com.

——"The Compassion of Truth in Biblical Perspective," [n.d.], at albertmohler.com/article_read.php?cid=7.

Montoya, Alex D., "The Church's Response to Homosexuality," *The Master's Seminary Journal*, 19:2 (2008), pp. 233–248.*

——"Homosexuality and the Church," *The Master's Seminary Journal*, 11:2 (2000), pp. 155–168.*

Nortje-Meyer, Lilly, "Critical Principles for a Homosexual Reading of Biblical Texts: An Introduction," *Scriptura*, 88 (2005), pp. 174–182.

Oberholzer, Pieter, "Gay Couples' Covenants with Each Other and God Exist, Regardless of Church Attitude," *The Cape Times*, August 17, 2004, p. 9.

Olasky, Marvin, "Mental Disorder to Civil-Rights Cause," *World Magazine*, February 19, 2005, pp. 30–32.

Osten, Craig, and **Sears, Alan,** *The Homosexual Agenda: Exposing the Principal Threat to Religious Freedom Today* (Nashville, TN: Broadman & Holman, 2003).*

Piper, John, "Marriage: A Matrix of Christian Hedonism," October 16, 1987, at desiringgod.org.

Select bibliography

——and **Grudem, Wayne,** (eds.), *Recovering Biblical Manhood & Womanhood: A Response to Evangelical Feminism* (Wheaton, IL: Crossway, 1991).

Plowman, Edward E., "Defining Moments: Efforts to Protect Marriage Continue to Gain Steam in the States," February 11, 2006, at worldmag.com.

Robertson, O. Palmer, *The Genesis of Sex: Sexual Relationships in the First Book of the Bible* (Phillipsburg, NJ: P & R, 2002).*

SAPA, "Sex, the Currency of Wayward Dutch Teens," November 11, 1008, at iol.co.za.

Satinover, Jeffery, MD, *Homosexuality and the Politics of Truth* (Grand Rapids, MI: Baker, 1996).*

Schmidt, Thomas E., *Straight and Narrow? Compassion and Clarity in the Homosexual Debate* (Leicester, UK: InterVarsity Press, 1995).*

Seow, Choon-Leong, (ed.), *Homosexuality and Christian Community* (Louisville, KY: Westminster John Knox Press, 1996).

Seu, Andrée, "Born that Way: If it Comes Naturally, Does it Mean it's not Sin?", November 6, 2004, at worldmag.com.

——"Connecting the Dots," December 23, 2003, at worldmag.com.

Shears, Jake, "When Elton Met Jake," November 12, 2006, at observer.guardian.co.uk.

Signorile, Michelangelo, "I Do, I Do, I Do, I Do, I Do," *OUT*, May 1996, pp. 30–32.

Smith, F. LaGard, *Sodom's Second Coming* (Eugene, OR: Harvest House, 1993).

Solimeo, Sergio Luiz, "The Animal Homosexuality Myth," accessed July 11, 2008, at narth.com.

Sprigg, Peter, *Outrage: How Gay Activists and Liberal Judges are Trashing Democracy to Redefine Marriage* (Washington: Regency, 2004).*

Sullivan, Andrew, (ed.), *Same-Sex Marriage: Pro and Con* (New York: Vintage, 1997).

Thatcher, Adrian, *Liberating Sex: A Christian Sexual Theology* (London, UK: SPCK, 1993).

Tozer, A. W., *The Knowledge of the Holy* (San Francisco: Harper & Row, 1978).

Turner, Dorie, "Lutheran Congregation Keeps Gay Pastor," accessed August 14, 2007, at hosted.ap.org/dynamic/stories/L/LUTHERANS_GAY_PASTOR?SITE=NCAGW&SECTION=HOME&TEMPLATE=DEFAULT.

Unruh, Bob, "'Mom,' 'Dad,' Targeted by California Bias Ban," September 12, 2007, at worldnetdaily.com/news/article.asp?ARTICLE_ID=57593.

Veith, Gene Edward, "The Nordic Track," March 6, 2004, at worldmag.com.

——"Wandering Shepherds," August 23, 2003, at worldmag.com.

Vincent, Lynn, "Remaining Silent: Canada: Parliament OKs a Law to Criminalize Speech Deemed 'Anti-Gay,'" May 8, 2004, at worldmag.com.

Welch, Edward T., "Homosexuality: Current Thinking and Biblical Guidelines," *The Journal of Biblical Counseling*, 13:3 (1995), pp. 19–29.

Wells, David F., *Losing our Virtue: Why the Church Must Recover its Moral Vision* (Grand Rapids, MI: Eerdmans, 1998).

White, Danielle, and **Kaplan, Jan,** "The State's Role in Supporting Marriage and Family Formation," accessed November 5, 2008, at financeproject.org/Publications/supportingmarriageandfamilyformationIN.htm.

White, James R., and **Jeffery D. Niell,** *The Same Sex Controversy* (Minneapolis: Bethany House, 2002).*

Wold, Donald J., *Out of Order: Homosexuality in the Bible and the Ancient Near East* (Grand Rapids, MI: Baker, 1998).

Wolfe, Christopher, "Born to be Defiled? Phony Science Posits 'Gay Gene Theory,'" May 20, 2000, at worldmag.com.

Young, Katherine K., and **Nathanson, Paul,** "Marriage à la Mode: Answering the Advocates of Gay Marriage," 2003, at marriageinstitute.ca.

About Day One:

Day One's threefold commitment:

- To be faithful to the Bible, God's inerrant, infallible Word;
- To be relevant to our modern generation;
- To be excellent in our publication standards.

I continue to be thankful for the publications of Day One. They are biblical; they have sound theology; and they are relevant to the issues at hand. The material is condensed and manageable while, at the same time, being complete—a challenging balance to find. We are happy in our ministry to make use of these excellent publications.

JOHN MACARTHUR, PASTOR-TEACHER, GRACE COMMUNITY CHURCH, CALIFORNIA

It is a great encouragement to see Day One making such excellent progress. Their publications are always biblical, accessible and attractively produced, with no compromise on quality. Long may their progress continue and increase!

JOHN BLANCHARD, AUTHOR, EVANGELIST AND APOLOGIST

Visit our website for more information and to request a free catalogue of our books.

www.dayone.co.uk

Homosexuality
Christian truth and love

PAUL E. BROWN (EDITOR)

160PP, TRADE PAPERBACK

ISBN 978–1–84625–054–5

Homosexuality has hardly been out of the news in the last few years. This book looks at the issue from the viewpoint of a Christian faith based squarely on the Bible. So two important chapters consider carefully what the Bible says about sexuality in general and then what it says about homosexual behaviour. But there is much more—including an examination of the attitude of the Christian church in history a look at homosexuality from a medical perspective. It reviews recent legislation, its possible impact upon Christians and churches, and gives some guidance on a Christian response. It covers the pastoral response in the local church and concludes with a testimony which introduces the work of True Freedom Trust. The Christian position is one which is now widely misunderstood and is often thought to be merely a matter of prejudice if not of actual animosity to homosexual people. But, so this book argues, it is a principled view which comes in the context of all that the Bible says about God and man, about truth and love and the gospel of grace.

Christian truth and love

EDITOR: PAUL E BROWN

Day One

CONTRIBUTORS

Paul E Brown is a retired pastor. Rev. Dr Kenneth Brownell is the pastor of East London Tabernacle Baptist Church and editor of the theological journal Foundations. Declan Flanagan is the Chief Executive of Rural Ministries. Martin Hallett is the Director of True freedom Trust, a Christian support and teaching ministry offering hope and help to men and women struggling with homosexuality, lesbianism and similar issues, and to their families and friends. Roger Hitchings is the pastor of East Leake Evangelical Church. Dr Peter Saunders is the General Secretary of the Christian Medical Fellowship.